P9-CKR-567

JUST FRIENDS

Also by the author

INTIMATE STRANGERS: Men and Women Together

WOMEN OF A CERTAIN AGE: The Midlife Search for Self

WORLDS OF PAIN: Life in the Working-Class Family

Just Friends

THE ROLE OF FRIENDSHIP IN OUR LIVES

Lillian B. Rubin

HARPER & ROW, PUBLISHERS, New York
Cambridge, Philadelphia, San Francisco, London
Mexico City, São Paulo, Singapore, Sydney

1817

Grateful acknowledgment is made to the following publishers for permission to reprint:

Lines from *The Elder Statesman* by T. S. Eliot. Copyright © 1959 by Thomas Stearns Eliot. Reprinted by permission of Farrar, Straus and Giroux, Inc., and Faber and Faber Ltd.

Lines from "The Death of the Hired Man" from *The Poetry of Robert Frost,* edited by Edward Connery Lathem. Copyright 1930, 1930, © 1969 by Holt, Rinehart and Winston. Copyright © 1958 by Robert Frost. Copyright © 1967 by Lesley Frost Ballantine. Reprinted by permission of Holt, Rinehart and Winston, Publishers, and Jonathan Cape Ltd.

 For information address Harper & Row, Publishers, Inc., 10 East 53rd Street, New York, N.Y. 10022. Published simultaneously in Canada by Fitzhenry & Whiteside Limited, Toronto.

FIRST EDITION

Designer: Sidney Feinberg

Library of Congress Cataloging in Publication Data

Rubin, Lillian B.

Just friends.

Bibliography: p.

Includes index.

1. Friendship. I. Title.

BF575.F66R83 1985 158'.25 84-43074

ISBN 0-06-015460-8

85 86 87 88 89 HC 10 9 8 7 6 5 4 3 2 1

For those dearest of friends:
Barbara, Dorothy, Kim and Michael

Those friends thou hast, and their adoption tried,
Grapple them to the soul with hoops of steel . . .

Hamlet

Contents

Acknowledgments

I am fortunate indeed to be able to start a book about friendship by acknowledging the contributions of friends without whom my work and my life would be infinitely poorer. For their patience in listening to me talk about the issues that preoccupied me during the course of researching and writing this book, and for their thoughtful reading of all or part of this work, my gratitude to Bob Alford, Lynnette Beall, Bob Cantor, Ani Chamichian, Diane Ehrensaft, Peter Finkelstein, Jacqueline Hackel, Arlie Hochschild, Terry Kupers, Joyce Lipkis, Richard Lucas, Anne Marcus, Karen Paige, Kurt Schlesinger, Roger Straus, Gladys Topkis.

Four others deserve special recognition. Barbara Artson, Kim Chernin, Dorothy Jones and Michael Rogin are friends whose lives and thoughts are so entangled with mine that it is impossible to weigh their contribution. With each of them I share a rare friendship; yet each is different from the other. All together, their sustained and intimate presence in my life has, for years, been a vital force in my own development, affecting not just this work but the quality of my life and thought. Thus this book is dedicated to them.

Terry Stein, a professor at Michigan State University who spent a sabbatical year working with me in the field, has earned my admiration and appreciation for the fine interviewing skills he brought to the task, for the many hours of fruitful discussion about the issues we were encountering and, not least, for the warm friendship that has blossomed in the ensuing years.

The idea for this book was born a long time ago in a dialogue with a special friend who was, at the time, also my publisher. To Erwin Glikes, who helped plant the seed and nurture it in infancy, a very special word of gratitude.

It is a pleasure to be able to give public acknowledgment once again to the contribution of my agent, Rhoda Weyr. Her friendship, support and wisdom have been invaluable throughout the writing of this book.

My editor, Hugh Van Dusen, has been an unfailing source of enthusiasm and encouragement. His sensitivity and his ability to grasp the nuance of my work and thought have made our relationship a pleasure. And Janet Goldstein has been a reassuring presence as she shepherded the manuscript through the publication process with quiet competence.

Through the years of my association with Harper & Row, many others have done their jobs with admirable dispatch and efficiency, providing the support every author needs to turn a manuscript into a book and to bring it before the public. All these people have names, but most of them are unknown to me. I want to take this opportunity to make my gratitude known to all of them—those whose names I know and those I don't—with a special note of thanks to the people with whom I've worked most closely: Ruth Brengel, Lisa Fillman, Marcia Harrison, Dan Harvey, Bill Shinker.

Jessina McGaugh has, for years, eased my life so that I could be freer to do my work—a gift for which I shall always be grateful.

The research for this book was originally supported by a three-year grant from the Behavioral Sciences Research Branch of the National Institute of Mental Health (MH 33624).

There is really no adequate way to thank the women and men who gave so generously of themselves and their time, spending hours talking to me about their lives and their friends. Without them, there would be no book. I hope, therefore, that I have succeeded in the task I set for myself—to honor not just the content of their words but the spirit in which they were told to me.

To Marcy, my daughter, whose friendship has that matchless quality possible only when kinship and friendship become one, my love and gratitude.

Last but surely not least, there is my husband, Hank Rubin. As always, he has shared intimately with me the triumphs and pains of writing a book. He read and reread every word I wrote, listened patiently as I tried out ideas, encouraged the good ones, helped me to abandon the bad ones, to reformulate those that had some promise. He rejoiced with me when it was going well, held my head and my hand when it wasn't, refusing to join me only in those moments of discouragement when I became anxious about my ability to do the job. He is not only my lover, my mate, my companion, but in the very deepest sense of the word, a friend without peer.

—LILLIAN RUBIN

El Cerrito, California
December 1, 1984

JUST FRIENDS

The Neglected Relationship

August 21, 1983. My best friend's son is about to be married —a young man I have known since he was a small boy.

It's uncharacteristically warm and bright for an August day in San Francisco, where summertime usually is accompanied by fog that cools the air and dims the spectacular views around the bay. But I'm not paying much attention to the brilliant day, for weddings are a time for reflection. And friendship, in particular, has engaged my reflective moments of late. So as we drive over the city's hills, I'm thinking about friendship—about the hundreds of interviews on the subject I have compiled over the past few years, about my own friendship with this young man and his family.

Barbara, his mother, and I have been "like sisters," only closer than most sisters. We have shared the mundane details of everyday life along with the extraordinary events, both painful and pleasurable, that happen only once in a while. We have, at times, moved apart in anger or hurt, and we have come together again—each of us unable in her own way to bear a permanent rupture in the relationship.

Because of the depth and intensity of our friendship, our families, too, have become entwined. Her husband and children are important in my life, just as mine are in hers. I've taken her kids to lunch or dinner, listened to their problems, soothed and smoothed the inevitable conflicts teen-agers and young adults have with parents. She and my daughter take time from busy professional lives for an occasional lunch just because they miss seeing each other.

One hundred and fifty people have been invited to the wedding—family, friends, acquaintances and associates of the bride and groom and their parents. As usual on such ceremonial occasions, except for the friends who attend the young couple, the separation between family and others, whether close friend or casual acquaintance, is clearly marked.[1] Special seating for the family, preferred status and open access to the celebrants, often some small part in the ceremony or the rituals surrounding it —all socially accepted and expected ways of affirming family solidarity, of honoring the uniqueness of family relationships, of setting them apart from all others.

Sometimes the actual relationships to which these rituals pay homage are especially close, and singling them out is a testament to their significance. Often they are not. Yet generally we don't question the customary arrangements, don't wonder why we bow to them, don't seriously consider alternatives. Or if we do, we hastily retreat in guilt and confusion, fearful of violating some primal covenant. Family members may have little contact in daily life, may even actively dislike each other, but at weddings and funerals they sit together in the family pew.

In my friend's family, there are no great tensions. She and her only sister have a warm relationship; Aunt Harriet is a beloved person in her nephew's life. So when she is given an honorific part in the post-ceremony ritual designed by the young couple, it seems perfectly appropriate, not something anyone would notice or comment on. Not anyone, that is, who isn't thinking about friendship and its meaning in our lives; not anyone who isn't also Barbara's best friend and the groom's surrogate aunt.

I notice. My attention is caught by the stark clarity of the line between family and friend. For the first time, I'm acutely aware of how undifferentiated I am from any of the other hundred or so friends and acquaintances in attendance.

I share my observations with my husband, who, in the moment, sees nothing unusual, certainly nothing to merit comment. "That's the way it usually goes, isn't it?" he replies. I comment to a mutual friend who can usually be counted on for some articulate response. But she only looks at me absently and, apparently not knowing what else to say, murmurs politely, "Mmmmmm, yes, I see." All of which reminds me how deeply entrenched are such ways of being and doing, how unquestioningly we accept the norms which separate friend and kin, which almost unfailingly give preferred status to relations of blood, which teach that "Blood is thicker than water."

I ask myself whether I'm just jealous of Harriet. I tell myself impatiently that there's no great social issue at stake here, that I'm just hurt by the fact that, on this public occasion, it's the real sister who is singled out while the significance of my friendship with Barbara remains a private understanding. Perhaps. But the word "just" rankles. Would Harriet have been jealous if the situation had been reversed? I think so! But who would trivialize her feelings with that word? Not I surely; for I would understand, as I believe most of us would.

A week or so later I have dinner with Barbara. We have talked on the telephone, of course, but this is the first time we have met since the wedding. So once again we talk about it, exchanging gossip, sharing our impressions of people and events. Choosing my words with care, I tell her also of my observations about how differently friend and kin are treated at such occasions. Despite my attempt to sound objective and to raise the discourse to a discussion of "such occasions," she goes right to the heart of the matter. "There's something else, isn't there? You have some feelings about Harriet's role."

I'm relieved in a way; she knows, too, that there's something awry here. But I'm also stung. If she knew, how did it happen that way, seemingly without thought? The problems that go into planning a wedding, of bringing together two strange families who are suddenly to be linked through their children, were discussed repeatedly in the months preceding the occasion. Why had she never spoken to me about this one?

With these thoughts jangling inside me, I hedge: "Not exactly. Actually I don't think I'd even have noticed if I hadn't been thinking about a focus for the friendship book." "But you did notice," she persists. "And obviously you have some feelings about it." Reluctantly I assent, then ask, "Who made that choice, you or Brad?" "I did," she says without hesitation. Then, reaching across the table to put a hand on mine. "I know what you must be thinking, but how could it have been otherwise? She's my sister!"

How indeed?

Friendship in our society is strictly a private affair. There are no social rituals, no public ceremonies to honor or celebrate friendships of any kind, from the closest to the most distant—not even a linguistic form that distinguishes the formal, impersonal relationship from the informal and personal one.

It's not that way everywhere. Some other Western cultures have rituals to mark the progress of a friendship and to give it public legitimacy and form. In Germany, for example, there's a small ceremony called *Duzen,* the name itself signifying the transformation in the relationship. The ritual calls for the two friends, each holding a glass of wine or beer, to entwine arms, thus bringing each other physically close, and to drink up after making a promise of eternal brotherhood with the word *Bruderschaft.* When it's over, the friends will have passed from a relationship that requires the formal *Sie* mode of address to the familiar *Du.* [2]

In our own society, no clear lines mark the beginnings of a friendship; often none mark the ending either. Relations of blood generally end in death—clear and unequivocal. But friendships usually just fade away. Beginnings are equally unambiguous in the family: A baby is born and instantly there are mother, father, sister, brother, aunts, uncles, cousins. With marriage also, beginnings and endings are strikingly clear: Marriages start with a wedding and end with death or divorce. But for us, friendship is a *non–event*—a relationship that just *becomes,* that grows, develops, waxes, wanes and, too often perhaps, ends, all without ceremony or ritual to give evidence of its existence.

Our language offers few possibilities for distinguishing among friendships, the word "friend" being used to refer to a wide range of relationships with varying degrees of closeness and distance. Compare this with kinship and the rich set of descriptive terms the language makes available. The words "mother," "father," "aunt," "uncle," "cousin," all tell us something specific about a person's place in the kin circle. Whether related by blood or by marriage, each relationship has its own designation. There's no ambiguity there; no questions nag us about who is a husband, a wife, a sibling, a child, a parent, a mother-in-law, a brother-in-law. We all know. We know, too, what to expect in those relationships because the rules and boundaries—however imperfectly articulated or realized, however much in flux in this historical moment—are, for most of us, more clearly understood and accepted with kin than they are with friends.

But what can we make of this dialogue with a thirty-two-year-old man who spoke with ease and authority about his "fifteen or twenty" intimate friends? No matter how much I probed or prodded, no matter how I phrased and rephrased the questions, he had all the "right" answers. "Yes, I can talk to them about anything, no matter what the problem is," he insisted. "Yes, I can turn to them in any kind of trouble." "Trust," he said, "and joint helpfulness"—these are the central and defining features of friendship for him. "Can you count on all these fifteen or twenty people to be trustworthy and helpful in any situation?" I asked. "Yes," he assured me, "I sure can."

"Do you have a best friend?" I asked him, as I had asked everyone else. "Sure do; he's a guy I've known since high school." "How often do you see each other?" Now the answers came with more hesitation. "Well, in fact, we haven't seen each other since he moved east about ten years ago." "How do you stay in touch; by phone?" "Yeah, well, actually, you see, we don't, not really; maybe a couple of times we talked on the phone since he left." "What makes him a best friend then?" I asked as I found myself becoming increasingly nonplussed. "It's just like I said—trust, that's what it is. I know I can absolutely trust him." "Trust him with what?" "With anything I need. I could land on his doorstep in the cold of winter and the dead of night and I know he'd be right there." Flippantly, and without really expecting any surprises in his answer, I wondered, "Just where is this doorstep on which you'd always be welcome to land?" A moment of silence and then, "I'm not sure. You see, he moved a while back and I don't know exactly where he lives now." "How far back?" "I don't remember exactly, a couple of years maybe."

Long-distance friendships are, of course, common in our mobile society, many of them representing deep and lasting ties. People speak often of the importance of such friendships, giving evidence of a connection that's undeniable, telling tales of how, after months of separation, they come together and pick up where they left off, as if no time had elapsed. These people, however, know where to find each other, certainly maintain contact more than once in ten years.

But I met others who told stories about friendships that, although less extreme than the tale just told, raised similar doubts. Consequently, in forty-four cases (15 percent of those interviewed), where the contradictions seemed very clear, I asked people to refer me on to all those they had named as close friends or best friends. I ended up with the names of 186 people, of whom I contacted 132—some in person, some, who lived in distant places, by telephone. These were relatively brief exchanges since I didn't mean to examine their friendship histories fully, only to discover if the designation of "close" or "best" friend was reciprocal.

The results? Eighty-four (64 percent) made no mention of the person I originally interviewed on their list of friends. Sometimes, when I prompted them, they would remember, expressing some mild discomfort at having forgotten this friend while also letting me know this was not an important relationship for them. But often they responded vaguely, acknowledging that they knew him or her but didn't think of the person as a friend. The remaining forty-eight people I contacted listed my respondent as a friend spontaneously, but in only eighteen cases (14 percent) did he or she come anywhere near the top of their list.[3]

We have friends, and we have "just" friends; we have good friends, and we have best friends. Yet such is the elusiveness of the idea of "friend" that not even the people involved can always say which is which.

"What is a friend?"—a question I asked everyone I talked with. The answers I heard varied somewhat depending on class, gender and generational perspectives. But regardless of the experienced reality of their lives and relationships, most people presented some idealized definition of friendship. *Trust, honesty, respect, commitment, safety, support, generosity, loyalty, mutuality, constancy, understanding, acceptance.* These are the most widely heralded qualities of friendship, the minimum requirements, if you will, to be counted as a friend.[4]

Nothing wrong with the list, of course. It just doesn't match up with the friends they described later in our discussion. Yet these are not simply distortions of fact. Rather they are at once the expression of the idealized imagery that talk about friends summons up and the widely shared wish for just such a relationship.

Just as with love, the *idea* of friendship stirs yearnings from our infantile past, bringing to life the hope that somewhere, sometime, perfect love, trust, security and safety will be ours once more. Therefore, when the talk turns abstract, as in "What is a friend?," rather than concrete, as in "What is your relationship with Jane like?," we're more likely to respond from the wish than from the reality.[5] It's then that the disparity between the idealized version of *friendship* and the reality of relations with *friends* stands revealed so clearly. It's then, too, that we can see that this paradox is itself a crucial and often overlooked dimension of this whole subject.

From the beginning, it was contradictions such as these that made this project alternately exhilarating and aggravating. For without institutional form, without a clearly defined set of norms for behavior or an agreed-upon set of reciprocal rights and obligations, without even a language that makes distinctions between the different kinds of relationships to which we apply the word, there can be no widely shared agreement about what is a friend. Thus it is that one person will claim as a friend someone who doesn't reciprocate; that another who has been called a good friend says, when I ask him about this relationship, "Oh, yeah, John, we worked together a year or so ago. Haven't seen him since."

Yet despite the ambiguity that surrounds friendship in this society, generations of American children have grown up under the influence of an adult world that has brooded more over their social adjustment than their moral development—indeed, often equated the two.[6] By the time a child is two, parents already are concerned about the little one's ability to be sociable, searching anxiously for signs that she or he will be successful in making friends. Soon after, teachers join parents in worrying about the child who spends "too much time alone" or who "has trouble relating to others."

Since from our earliest childhood, we have been judged and measured by our ability to make and keep friends, friendship, for us, is not *just* something to be desired. To be without friends is a cause for shame, a stigma, a symptom of personal deficiency that none of us takes lightly.[7] Indeed, in notable ways, our very sense of ourselves is connected to our ability to negotiate the world of friendship. Consequently, the lack of friends can torment even very small children, leaving them with feelings that range from a sense of personal inadequacy to a wish to die. In

The Social World of the Child, William Damon tells of the eight-year-old girl who said she would "feel like killing [herself]" if she didn't have friends.[8]

Who among us has forgotten the agony of standing alone in the schoolyard when others had friends with whom to play? Who cannot recall the youthful dread of being unpopular? Who today can find oneself alone at a cocktail party without discomfort, without being shadowed by the anxieties of the past?

Yet until very recently, the subject of adult friendship has been largely absent from the literature of the social and psychological sciences, getting little more than passing reference in studies devoted to other issues. Indeed, so blind have we been to the social and psychological meanings of friendship that anthropologists, trained in the art of studying alien cultures, have paid scant attention to these relationships, even in societies where rituals exist and institutional forms are quite obvious.[9]

Our well-developed ideology about marriage and the family, our insistence that these are the relationships that count for the long haul, have, I believe, blinded us to the meaning and importance of friendship in our lives. Until the soaring divorce rate pointed so sharply to a crisis in marriage, we still expected that all our needs for emotional intimacy, social connectedness and intellectual stimulation would be met there. Today we know better. But the knowledge of this reality, no matter how powerfully it has made itself felt, has failed to correct the fantasy.

To understand why, we must look to the nuclear family itself —to the many ways it perpetuates itself, not least by creating a set of needs for the kind of intense emotional bonds that are formed there.[10] The isolation of the nuclear family, the privacy of this "sanctum into whose hallowed chambers no outsider has a right of entry,"[11] means that it is not just the primary source of survival for the dependent infant, but the wellspring of emotional gratification and identification for the developing child as well.

We know, of course, that the emotional needs of infancy and

childhood often are not adequately met in the family. Nevertheless, these old emotional connections live inside us with powerful intensity—silken threads that bind us more tightly than any chains. Consequently, we are left forever hungry to feel again the depth of the bond we once knew, to find a new love within which we can experience these old feelings once more. We don't wholly ignore friends, of course. But usually they are a distant second, their place in our lives contingent upon the demands and vicissitudes of love and marriage.

The last few years have seen a quickening of interest in friendship among adults, however, an emerging awareness about the importance of friends in our lives. The slim body of existing research tells us that, even where supportive and solid family relationships exist, friends count in any number of ways —from playmates to soul mates. Robert Weiss, who has written extensively on the subject of loneliness, presents convincing evidence that, even when people are comfortably and happily married, the absence of friends exacts a heavy cost in loneliness and isolation.[12] Other studies have found that friends and neighbors provide a more effective support network for schizophrenic women living at home than do members of their family;[13] that friends are more important for maintaining morale in old age than are grandchildren;[14] that divorced women get help with the practical aspects of living from kin, but friends are crucial for the emotional support they offer and the link to the outside world they provide.[15]

In another vein, social scientists, worrying about the anomie and alienation of urban life, have brought forth a body of work examining the social networks within which people's lives are embedded.[16] Feminist scholars, attempting to redress the omissions of the past, have produced a small literature showing that women's friendships have always been an important part of their lives and thoughts.[17]

Outside the academy as well, several of the major institutions of our society seem to have found their voice on the subject. Look, for example, at the spate of articles about friendship that have recently preoccupied the newspapers and mass-circulation magazines.[18] Notice the major national advertising campaign of the telephone company which exhorts us to "reach out and touch someone," while it shows old and young alike finding new joy in life through a phone call from a friend. In New York City, the telephone company has actually instituted a "Phone-A-Friend" service, in which people who don't have friends of their own can dial a number that will connect them to lonely strangers like themselves.[19] And in northern California, Pacific Bell has just announced a service called Talkline—a program offering teen-agers, adults and seniors their own special numbers that allow them to join a conversation with as many as ten others, all unknown.

Even the California State Department of Health has gotten into the act with a series of public service announcements on radio and television extolling the value of friendship for our physical and mental health. "Make a friend," these ads urge. "Friends can be good medicine." Yet the very need for such a campaign is testimony to the ambivalence and ambiguity with which friendship is held in our society. For on the one hand, it tells us that friendship remains our neglected relationship while, at the same time, acknowledging that from early childhood right on up through old age, friends are crucial to our well-being.[20]

To study friendship, then, is to trip over the ambiguity, ambivalence, contradiction and paradox with which this subject is hedged in our society—a fact the pages that follow will document repeatedly. But this ambiguity is only of interest in the context of some larger understandings about the meaning and purpose friends have in our lives.

On these same pages, therefore, I shall argue also that friends are central actors in the continuing developmental drama of our adulthood. The burgeoning field of adult development contradicts earlier theories that identity formation is a one-time, all-or-nothing affair that is crystallized in early childhood and determined by the nature of family relations.[21] Rather, most modern theorists now understand the formation of a personal identity as a lifetime process to which our varied experiences in the larger social world, as well as in the family, make their contributions—a process, both conscious and unconscious, in which each of us acts as mediator, in which the experience of the external world is given internal substance and meaning by our own particular integrative and interpretive capacities.

From birth onward, we are active and seeking participants in our own development—seeking, in that we continually respond to our internal need for connection with another; active, in that we are in a constant process of internalizing representations of people and objects from the world around us. Our sense of self is formed through this process of internalizing the external world, which, among other things, means making attachments and identifications with others who touch our lives.[22]

This is how we come to know who and what we are in the world. Through our connection with others, we develop our sense of our common humanity. Through the images we internalize from the world around us, we eventually take our own measure. A sense of self and personal identity is formed and sharpened in the context of such human interaction—products of the interplay between external and internal, between social experience and its psychological elaboration.

In this process, friends count. Indeed, it is the central thesis of this book that our friendships and our developing sense of ourselves are in a complex and continuing interaction, each influencing the other in ways we have not, until now, fully understood. On the one hand, friends have a powerful effect on the development of a full, coherent and satisfactory sense of self; and on the other, the identifications of our earliest childhood years, and the sense of self that grows from them, affect the kinds of friendships we are likely to form in adulthood.

Whether child or adult, it is friends who provide a reference outside the family against which to measure and judge ourselves; who help us during passages that require our separation and individuation; who support us as we adapt to new roles and new rules; who heal the hurts and make good the deficits of other relationships in our lives; who offer the place and encouragement for the development of parts of self that, for whatever reasons, are inaccessible in the family context. It's with friends that we test our sense of self-in-the-world, that our often inchoate, intuitive, unarticulated vision of the possibilities of a self-yet-to-become finds expression.

In all these ways and more, friendship, as we shall see, finds its long-neglected place in the drama of human development. But since friendships don't exist in isolation from other important relationships in our lives, in particular those in our nuclear and extended families, we start with a comparison of kinship and friendship.

About the Study

This book is based on in-depth interviews, each lasting several hours, with three hundred men and women, ages twenty-five to fifty-five—people who run the gamut from high-school dropout to college professor, who are single and married, working class and middle class. About two-thirds come from California, where I live and work; the rest are distributed among urban centers across the country. The class composition of the sample is: 22 percent professional upper middle class; 40 percent middle class; 38 percent working class. Class background was determined by a combination of education and occupation.

I have, in addition, one hundred interviews with homosexual men and lesbians which focus on their love relationships, their friendships, and the interaction between the two. But since homosexuality raises particular issues around friendship, whether same-sex or cross-sex—issues that deserve a book in their own right—throughout this book I will use these interviews for comparative purposes in specific instances only.

Because I was interested in how friendship outside a marriage can affect life inside it, I talked with both partners. Because I wanted to understand friendship from all sides of the interaction, I often interviewed one or more of the people a respondent designated as friends. Wherever possible, I talked to those who were named as best friends. But I did not limit myself to this category alone. Sometimes also I sought out someone who was called a good friend, sometimes someone who was "just a friend," the decision based on what seemed either most problematic or most interesting in the original interview.

Right from the beginning, the paradoxical nature of the whole subject of friendship in our society became clear. There was no resistance to participating in the study; indeed, quite the contrary. It made no difference who they were or where they lived; all eagerly granted my request for an interview. But such are the contradictions, both conscious and unconscious, people experience around this issue that it was often harder for them to sort out their friendships, and to speak openly and directly about them, than to dicuss the highly personal issues of family life that were the focus of my earlier studies, including even such intimate matters as sexual relations.

2

On Kinship and Friendship

Kin and friend—each important enough in the history of human relations to be the subject of a rich and complex lore, a curious mélange of the best and the worst in both relationships. The Roman philosopher Cicero wrote of a friend as "a second self,"[1] while the seventeenth-century poet Robert Burton warned that "Old friends become bitter enemies on a sudden for toys and small offenses."[2] Aristotle described friendship as "A single soul dwelling in two bodies,"[3] and believed that "Without friends no one would choose to live, though he had all other goods."[4] But Mark Twain commented acidly, "The holy passion of Friendship is of so sweet and steady and loyal and enduring a nature that it will last through a whole lifetime, if not asked to lend money."[5] Emerson said, "A friend may well be reckoned the masterpiece of nature,"[6] while in *The Devil's Dictionary,* Ambrose Bierce defined friendship as "A Ship big enough to carry two in fair weather, but only one in foul."[7] And the late President Harry Truman is reported to have quipped, "You want a friend for life, get a dog."

It is thus throughout the literature of friendship—romantic visions mingling with cynical ones, fears of treachery lying just below the surface of odes to love and loyalty. Shakespeare's *Julius Caesar* epitomizes the split, our own anxieties about disappointment and betrayal captured in Caesar's dying "Et tu, Brute!"

Kin relations, too, traditionally have generated their own combination of fear, anger, hope and fantasy. Thus, while an old Spanish proverb warned, "Between brothers, two witnesses and a notary," T. S. Eliot rhapsodized, "There's no vocabulary / For love within a family, love that's lived in / But not looked at, love within the light of which / All other love finds speech. / This love is silent."[8] A far cry from Samuel Butler's belief that "more unhappiness comes from this source [the family] than from any other—I mean from the attempt to prolong family connections unduly and to make people hang together artificially who would never naturally do so."[9]

Most anthropologists today argue that kinship is as much an *idea*—a system of belief—as it is a biological fact, and that the biological and social relationships need not necessarily coincide.[10] Kinship, they tell us, is defined in a social context, with different societies honoring different kin relationships.[11]

In some African societies, for example, a woman may enter a marriage with another woman, while a man is assigned the role of lover. When children are born, the female "husband" becomes their father, taking on the rights and obligations of the role exactly as if these were relations of blood. The biological father may continue as lover, but he remains outside the family circle and the immediate privileges and responsibilities it entails.[12]

Closer to home we have the families of the Mafia, which include kin linked by blood and marriage along with what anthropologists call "fictive kin"—that is, those who are not related by birth or marriage yet become part of the kin network.[13] And of course, both marriage and legal adoption routinely transform stranger into kin.

In the research for this book, one thing quickly became clear: *The idea of kin is so deeply and powerfully rooted within us that it is the most common metaphor for describing closeness.* No matter what the age, the life stage, the marital status or the sexual orientation, when people wanted to impress upon me the importance of their friendships and the quality of closeness, they invoked the metaphor of the family. "How can I tell you what my friends mean to me? They're like family"—words spoken over and over again.

As the nuclear family increasingly turned in on itself over the last century and a half, it became the primary source of emotional sustenance for its members.[14] Therefore, "family" for most urban adults in our society generally means the immediate members of the family of origin and, if married, the spouse and children of the family of procreation. But when invoking the family metaphor in speaking about friends, most people quite clearly mean the family into which they were born. Thus, when I asked people to speak with me about the quality of their family relationships, almost always the talk turned to parents and siblings. Of the three hundred women and men I interviewed, only twenty-four (8 percent) even mentioned aunts, uncles or cousins; fewer still called them significant.

Often my questions about relations with kin brought forth an almost reflexive response about closeness and devotion, only to have the other side surface, sometimes in the very next sentence. So, for example, a fifty-year-old businesswoman who started our conversation about her sister by saying, "I consider her my friend," went on to add:

> I'd do anything for her, but I don't share much with her in the way of confidences or what's really happening in my life or my thoughts. And I don't look to her for any advice or [*with some hesitation*] . . . for anything else really. In fact, we don't have a lot in common.

And the same people who said their friends are "as close as blood relations" frequently also said of these very relations, "I wouldn't pick them for people I want to spend time with, but what the hell, it's family." Or, "We get along all right, but we don't ask much of each other."

What does it mean, then, when friends are described as "like family"? Clearly the metaphor is meant to suggest something about the importance of the relationship—an intensity of connection, a sense of belonging, of continuity, of security. Yet as our discussions continued, most people began to comment also on the differences in the ways these two sets of relationships are experienced—differences that pointed to the contradictions and paradoxes in each of them.

"Can you tell me," I asked all those who spoke of friends as family, "what differences, if any, do you see in your relationships with friends and family?"

Almost all talked spontaneously and at length about the issue of self-disclosure—about how much more easily they can share important parts of themselves with friend than with kin, about how much less judgmental friends are about how they live, what they think, indeed, even who they are. Repeatedly, men and women told me that they value friends because, in contrast to family, "They accept me for who I am." A thirty-five-year-old lesbian, who lives two thousand miles from a family she said she "loves deeply" and would "do anything for," spoke about the difficulties she experiences in "being myself" with them.

> With family, they're so involved in your life—I mean in who you are and how you're living—that there's a kind of censorship with them that I don't feel with my friends. Especially with my parents, there's no point in telling them things about myself that I know would hurt them or upset them. Jesus, when I think about it, it's incredible; it took six years before I could tell them I'm lesbian. Everybody in the world knew but them.

How they present themselves in the family is, without doubt, a more acute problem among homosexual men and lesbians because of the stigma that still attaches to homosexuality and the consequent upheaval, if not outright rejection, that usually accompanies the "coming out" process. But even among people who live perfectly traditional lives, there's no dearth of talk about how they censor not only certain facts of their lives but their very presentation of self.

Yet as our discussions continued and the context shifted, I saw that this is only one part of the picture. Then, even many of those who insisted most vehemently, "I can be myself with friends in ways that are impossible with my family," spoke also of the ways in which they tend to treat friends more gingerly and tenderly than family, to show their shadow side to a parent or sibling more readily than to a friend, to risk conflict more easily with kin than with anyone outside the fold. Indeed, it soon became clear to me that there is almost nothing that people would say about either friendship or kinship—about the reasons why they're valued, about the levels of commitment, loyalty, obligation or expectation—that would not also be contradicted. Musing about these two sets of relationships and the contradictions each seemed to embody, a forty-one-year-old housewife said:

> I always like to think I can be as easy with my friends as I am with my family. And in some ways, it's certainly true—easier, in fact. There are things my friends know about me that I would never share with any member of my family. There's no doubt that, in many ways, my closest friends know me much better than my sister does. [*Then, after a pause in which she sat quietly, trying to formulate the rest of her thoughts*] But then there's a way she knows other things about me that I don't show my friends. I can be angry and impatient with her and holler at her, which I wouldn't do with friends. If I don't like something she says or does, I can get pretty mean and miserable sometimes. With friends you're more careful about showing that stuff. So maybe I'm really more honestly myself with my sister. It's confusing, isn't it?

The issue, however, is not honesty in the relationship, nor is it that we can be closer or more intimate in one set of relations than in another. Rather we experience these relationships differently; therefore, they tap a different set of responses.

Because our kin relations rest on the bonds forged in our earliest childhood years, they have an elemental quality that touches the deepest layers of our inner life and stirs our most primitive emotional responses. Therefore, we are likely to find these relationships more tumultuous than our friendships.

At the same time, partly because kin relationships have demonstrated their capacity to survive the storms of family life, partly just because we exist in the world as members of the same family, we experience these relationships with a sense of permanence that none other can match. Consequently, we have a greater sense of entitlement with kin than with friend, a greater sense of security, even in the face of behaviors that we know to be unacceptable anywhere else.

It's not, I hasten to add, that other relationships are wholly free of the primitive emotional responses we experience with kin. Any close relationship, whether with a mate, a lover or a friend, has the potential to recreate within us some of the same feelings of rivalry we had with a sibling, the same separation struggle we engaged with a parent, the same dependency needs, the same vulnerability, the same conflicts, the same ambivalence.

These feelings will be contained more or less easily, depending upon the relationship and the expectations that are given legitimacy within it. In a marriage, where lives and fortunes are tied together so profoundly, where children are shared, where the expression of dependency needs is encouraged and vulnerability expected, the primitive feelings generally will be more intensely felt than in a friendship.

While some people spoke of sparing friends the less attractive parts of themselves, others told of feeling the need to protect family members from knowing of their problems in a way that their friendships don't require. Talking about the anxiety of his family over his recent separation from an eight-year marriage, a thirty-one-year-old longshoreman said:

> You'd think it's their life that's just fallen apart instead of mine. They're upset all the time; they worry about me and my kids; they worry that I'm setting a bad example for my younger brothers. Okay, so I know all the noise is because they care. But who needs it! It winds up I'm trying to protect them because it's no help to have them know what I'm going through.

But this, too, tells only one side of the story. In reality, most of us are both *more* and *less* protective in our relations with kin compared to those with friends. Certainly a divorce creates problems for friends who are expected to stand by, not infrequently to take sides as well. Certainly it's hard for friends to watch another suffer and to experience their own helplessness. But because the boundaries between friends are clearer than they are between kin, there's no threat to self and identity in a friend's divorce. It is, after all, just another divorce—one among many.

For the family it's different. A child's divorce is a unique event that arouses a complex emotional response in a parent. There's anger at the disruption of the established family relations—"Think of the children!" There's the agony of self-doubt —"What did we do wrong?" There's the pain of watching a child, even an adult child, suffer—"I'd rather hurt myself." And overriding it all is the belief, often real enough, that this is not just the problem of the divorcing couple and their children but one that will have long-term consequences in the lives of all the members of the family.

For all these reasons, it's easier for friends to extricate themselves from the morass than it is for kin, easier to maintain enough distance from both the painful event and their feelings about it so as not to get hooked the way family members can. Friends, therefore, can be more helpful in such moments, not requiring that we protect them from the depth and intensity of our misery.

At the same time, there's a limit to what we expect from friends, a certain amount of care with which we approach them and ask for their help. So while many people I met said, "I'd go to my friends for anything, with any kind of problem," at another moment in our conversation, they said with equal conviction, "The family is the bottom line, the people you know you can always count on, no matter what." For whatever our anger or disillusion with our own families, however we may have known the failure of love or understanding there, friendship, for most of us, is experienced as a conditional relationship, kinship as an unconditional one. As Robert Frost wrote with such grace and economy, "Home is the place where, when you have to go there, / They have to take you in."[15]

Friends *choose* to do what kin are *obliged* to do. With friends, we must earn the rights and privileges that with family usually come just for being part of the collectivity. Thus kin still seem to most of us to offer a safe retreat, an anchor in an uncertain and unsteady world—the people who can be counted on when need is most urgent. Kinship still is most closely associated with words like "continuity," "stability," "trust," still summons images of abiding commitment, the promise of forever—what anthropologist David Schneider calls a "diffuse, enduring solidarity."[16] As a thirty-eight-year-old physical therapist said:

> The difference between friends and family is the sense of permanence in the relationship. I wish it weren't so, but the reality is that friendships can end or go through very drastic and disappointing changes. That doesn't happen with family. It doesn't end. And by the time you're an adult, you pretty well know what you can expect from them, so there aren't many surprises or disappointments.

With family, "it doesn't end"—a sharp reminder that without the commitments and obligations of blood, friendships require a level of care and attention for their maintenance in ways that kin do not. There's no obligation to take a friend or to keep one; we're free to choose without support or coercion from any quarter outside ourselves.

It's this very quality of friendship that is at once so powerfully seductive and so anxiety-provoking, indeed that is both its strength and its weakness. To be able to choose is to be free; to be chosen is to feel loved and admired. But in this, as in other arenas of living, freedom exacts its price in our sense of certainty and security. For what is given freely can be taken away with impunity as well. If we can be chosen, we can also be "*un*chosen."

Thus generally it's true that friends accept each other so long as they both remain essentially the same as they were when they met, or change in similar directions. If they change or grow in different or incompatible ways, the friendship most likely will be lost. We see the process at work most clearly in social or political movements—the "comrades" of the Old Left, for example, whose comradeship ended abruptly and bitterly when the beliefs and values that brought them together were no longer shared; or the draft resisters of the 1960s who found that their friends changed along with their views.[17]

Sometimes the decision to let a friendship die is unilateral. One member of the pair decides there's not enough common ground left to sustain the relationship, while the other can't figure out why they don't see each other anymore. At other times the decision to part is shared. People who were friends drift apart by mutual consent, both recognizing that the cement that held them together has disintegrated.

But kin relations usually don't just slip out of our lives with little notice. Most family ruptures are accompanied by plenty of noise—by years of struggle, by pleas and warnings, by threats and fights, by words spoken and regretted. Even when, in the heat of anger, a parent or child says, "I never want to see you again," this particular "never" can be quite short-lived. But whether a rift between family members is long-lasting or not, these relationships are not easily forgotten, as anyone knows who has had to deal with the guilt and pain the schism can call up no matter how many years have passed.

In my clinical practice, I listen repeatedly as men and women struggle with family conflicts they cannot put aside. A man with a lifelong history of antagonism toward his brother spends untold hours trying to cope with his guilt. A woman who, for years, has spoken only words of hate about a sister feels deeply hurt when some small effort at reconciliation is not reciprocated. A man who tells endless stories of humiliations by a father, who refused to see him for years, rushes anxiously to his father's bedside at the news of his illness. A woman who was an abused and beaten child, whose anger at her mother is incalculable, and who is herself married, with two children, weeps, on hearing the news of her mother's heart attack, "If she dies, it feels like I'll be all alone."

"You can pick your friends but not your relatives," we sigh with resignation, reminding ourselves that we have little choice in kin relationships, that there's nothing much we can do to change them. But let a friend commit offenses that are far less than the wounds family members can visit upon one another, and the friendship is very likely to be at stake.

"Would you try as hard to make a friendship work as you have with your relationships with your parents and your brother?" I asked a woman who talked about the difficulties in these kin relations. Laughing, she replied:

> It's true I've had to work very hard with my family in order to have any kind of relationship with them. But since I can pick my friends, I wouldn't have people like them for friends, so I wouldn't have to work so hard. I'd never keep a friend who can't see me as I am and like me for myself. With friends you start out really liking each other, otherwise you don't become friends. And when the liking's gone, so is the friendship. But with family you get strung together by accident, and then you

have to figure out a way to make what's imperfect and difficult to begin with tolerable.

"It's really just comes down to a blood tie and a shared history; that's what family is about," insisted one of the men I interviewed.

A shared history. Who else has always been there? Who else shares the memories? Who else was part of our earliest struggles and joys and pains? We can tell others about the events of our lives, about how we felt then, but only the members of our immediate family lived them with us.

This shared experience is an important basis for family solidarity, as we'll hear at any family gathering in the many conversations that start with "Remember when . . ." The consciousness of this shared history and its importance came up repeatedly as people struggled to understand their ambivalent, contradictory and ambiguous feelings about their relations with kin. Speaking of his older brother, one thirty-six-year-old chemist said:

> He was there when I was born, and he's been there ever since. He was my big brother, and I thought he was great when we were kids. I wanted to be just like him. He taught me how to play baseball; he let me tag after him. Maybe there's not a lot between us right now, but those things won't ever change. We shared more than a room. We shared a house and parents and a whole life. Now you can't beat that, can you?

And after telling of the "to-the-death battle" with her brother in their early childhood, a thirty-four-year-old university professor tried to explain the special quality of their connection in adulthood:

> It's the shared experience that makes for a kind of closeness that's different than with friends. There's a special sense, even if it's not always the kind of intimacy you have with a close friend, that comes with sharing that much, with having so many shared memories—this house and that dog, and a mutual relationship to parents. And we look like each other too. There's something there

that's intangible. Imagine, someone who's recognizably your brother; that's pretty special.

The ties that bind us to our nuclear family with such extraordinary tenacity, however, are not an unmixed blessing. On the one hand, they do, in fact, mean a certain security in the durability of these relationships. On the other hand, too often they are a force for inhibiting our development rather than facilitating it.[18]

Our identification with kin, and theirs with us, sets us up for a continual struggle both with them and with the regressive forces inside us. Just as some part of our sense of ourselves remains connected to who our family members are and how they behave in the world, they have an equally heavy investment in who we are and how we live, in ways that our friends do not. Partly as a way of affirming themselves, and partly as repayment for the years of struggle and sacrifice in raising a child, parents usually expect a certain type of "product." When they don't get it, their expressions of disapproval and disappointment can touch the most childlike parts of ourselves in ways that make us want to flee for our adult lives.

On our side, even when we're forty, parents can do or say something that will dicomfit us, throwing us back to those excruciating teen-age years when their very presence before our friends made us squirm with embarrassment. A good friend might also do something in public to disconcert us, of course. But because our identification with a friend is less profound than with kin, our response is less intense, more tolerant. Just so, where a crime committed by a friend—theft, murder, rape, child abuse—will inspire distaste or even disgust, the same act by a sibling or a mate will call up shame. We can fully dissociate from the friend; we can divorce the mate,[19] but the sibling is ours for life, even if we never see him or her again.

Thus, watching an adult family gathering is often like being witness to a reunion of young children and their parents.

Whether between sibs or between parent and child, archaic yearnings, ancient disappointments, old jealousies lie in wait, to be summoned up quickly and often unpredictably for reasons no one on the outside would understand.

Even well into adulthood, we can go "home" and find ourselves behaving in ways we left behind years ago. It's not just the parents who forget that a son or daughter is forty-five; the "child" forgets too. It's not just the parents who want the child to return, even if for just an hour or so; the adult child is not without some ambivalence about the regressive pulls that live inside him or her.

Often, of course, it's a nuisance to be treated like a child in adulthood—to be told what to do, what to wear, how to live. But there's also something warmly reassuring about the fact that this, at least, hasn't changed, that there's still a place where the child inside, even the naughty child, is welcomed, as these words from a thirty-six-year-old computer technician show:

> Sometimes I can get off on being treated like their little boy and knowing they like taking care of me. It's even okay when my mother tells me to go wash my hands before I come to the table.

But, as is true of most of us, he can tolerate his regressive wishes in small doses only. Soon his pleasure gives way to irritation and anxiety as the old conflicts of his struggle toward the development of a separate and autonomous self are called to the fore:

> There's always some things that go on with the family that make me get thrown back into acting like a damned teen-ager with them. I care about them a lot but, boy, it's hard as hell to get away from being a kid with them. None of that old garbage goes on with my friends, so I feel more like my real self with them, more substantial, than with the family.

Friendships, of course, are not entirely free of regressive pulls, especially when the relationship is very close. A friend can tap our wish to be mothered, can stimulate the jealousies and rivalries of our childhood years. Indeed, often we unconsciously choose friends because, with them, we experience once again something of the intensity of those early relationships, because they reawaken some of the same desires, the same conflicts.

Sometimes such a friendship offers the opportunity to master those old conflicts; sometimes we just replay them over and over again. But whatever the basis for the beginning of the relationship, there's little doubt that, if a friendship is to survive and grow, it will usually serve us better in keeping us in touch with our adult self than do our relations in the family. Comparing her relationships with friends and family on just this issue, a forty-five-year-old real estate agent talked about these differences and the consequences to her sense of herself:

> It's interesting to think about what I really value in my friends. It has something to do with liking myself better with them, especially when I compare it to how I can be with my brother or my parents.
>
> Let's see if I can make it come out right. [*Thinking awhile*] There's a way that family will accept you more than friends, but I don't know if that's so wonderful for you. I mean, it's not so good for your adult side to have people so accepting of the kid parts of you. It encourages you to let go of parts of yourself that you'd be a lot better off restraining.

It's not *just* a matter of the family accepting "the kid parts," however, true though that may be. It's also that the shared history, which consoles and reassures us with kin, too often disables them from seeing the person who lives today. In other settings, the "new" person is seen, understood and validated. Indeed, this is one of the most valued gifts friends offer us—a reflection of the self we most want to be. In the family it's different. There, it's our former selves that are entrenched in both the family's vision and our own. There, their old expectations meet our old needs for the love and acceptance that were once so important to our very survival. All together, they still have the power to entrap us.

Family members can see before them the adult who is now a family therapist and remember the child who was known as the troublemaker. They look at the person who is a fine tennis player and recall the child who was the clumsy *klutz*. The adult who is now the life of the party was once a shy and quiet child —a continuing source of comment and disbelief in the family. The unattractive child may be quite lovely now, but today's reality is filtered through yesterday's memory. And so it goes. No matter what the accomplishments of later life, the labels of childhood stick.

In families, too, each person tends to be assigned a place and a function. One child is said to be "just like Aunt Mary," another the "living image of Uncle John"; one is labeled the quiet, easygoing one, another stubborn and difficult; one is generous, another selfish; one is mom's child, another is claimed by dad. Designations and role assignments that, all too often, resist change no matter how old we get or how often we try to show another face.

Sometimes the way we're defined in the family is a wholly inaccurate reflection of who we are. More likely these characterizations address only one part of ourselves, the other parts being invisible or ignored in the family context. The generous gestures of the child who is defined as the selfish one, for example, go unnoticed and unrewarded. Whatever the reality, however, these designations often take on the quality of a self-fulfilling prophecy. We *become* what they say we are, at least when we are in their presence.

This "remembrance of things past" is also part of the underlying possessiveness that is so common to family relations—a perhaps unconscious but nevertheless vigorous attempt to tie us to our past, to activate the regressive side that longs to be a child again. For change threatens to unsettle existing relationships.

And even when those relationships have been less than satisfactory, family members move intuitively and often unconsciously to reestablish the old balance, as any family therapist sees all too often.[20]

To see ourselves without this baggage of the past, to affirm the reality of our adult selves—for this we turn to friends. But friendship and kinship are often in conflict. When children are small, parents fret if they don't get along well enough with others, aren't as socially adaptable as the parents would wish. As the children grow older and express that adaptability in their conformity to peer group norms, the same parents react with angry concern. Speaking about her parents' contradictory injunctions when she was a teen-ager, a thirty-three-year-old secretary complained:

> I never could figure out what they wanted. I was supposed to be Miss Popularity and to "retain my independent spirit"—by which they meant I was supposed to listen to them, not my friends.

When, as adults, the children develop real intimacies outside the family, parents often become jealous of those relationships, letting their offspring know that, despite the messages of a lifetime about the importance of friends, the unspoken rule is "family comes first."

Thus, just as most of us feel a singular obligation, if not commitment, to kin, family members operate on the assumption of special entitlement, believing that, by virtue of the relationship alone, they are owed particular privilege and attention. And like it or not, we usually grant them, often at some cost to our friendships. A twenty-nine-year-old single woman, an administrative assistant, talked about the bind she feels when she must choose:

> I have a very tight group of friends and they're really important to me—the mainstay of my life, you could say. Some of them don't

> have family around, and they think we all ought to make an effort to spend at least one of the big holidays together, Thanksgiving or Christmas. But in my family, it's not even something you could raise as a question for discussion. I'm just *expected* to be there. You're allowed not to be there if you have your own family; like my sister doesn't come to *all* the holidays because she has to go to her husband's family sometimes. That they understand. I don't mean they like it; they don't. But it's an excuse they can accept, the only one.

"Have you ever tried having a frank discussion about your wishes with your parents?" I asked.

> Not really. I tried a couple of times to hint, but they won't even hear. My mom's not dumb; she knows what I'm trying to talk about. But it's like she pretends not to get it so she won't have to deal with it. She just says something like, "You can bring your friends home, so what's the problem?" She'd never understand if I tried to tell her that my friends are like another family and I want to spend Christmas with just them. I can't get myself to hurt her that way even though I know I hurt my friends too. But it's different; they're more understanding.

The issue, it seems to me, is that, for most of us, kinship falls into the realm of the sacred, friendship into the arena of the secular. There's a mystique about kin relations, a sense of awe about them, a belief that these relationships, although not necessarily the people themselves, transcend ordinary considerations and everyday feelings. Indeed, it may not be the woman who is mother, the man who is father, to whom we pay homage. Rather it's to the *idea* of mother and father—to what those words stand for in consciousness, to the deep desires they stir in the unconscious parts of ourselves. In this sense, the same feelings that impel us into the church on Sunday morning move us toward the family visit in the afternoon. We do our duty to God and to family; we pay our debts; we relieve our guilt.

Certainly there are times and situations in which we are moved by more than reverence, obligation or guilt. Certainly there may be real love and honest pleasure in our relations with our family. But even when our most immediate and profound emotional connections are with friends, they will often take second place to the call of kin. Speaking of his intimate friendship with the sister of his ex-wife, a forty-year-old attorney registered just this understanding in words that underscore how much we tend to take for granted the sacredness of kin relations:

> I know the quality of my relationship with Kathy is much better and richer than her relationship with her sister, who's my ex-wife. We like to do the same things, and we share our lives in many ways. And there isn't the kind of rivalry between us that there is between her and her sister. Yet she's made it very clear to me that if her sister found our friendship too hard to handle and she had to make a choice between us, I'd fall by the wayside.

"You say that so calmly. Wouldn't that be hard for you?" I asked.

> Sure it would be hard. But it's what most people would do, I imagine. The choice isn't made in terms of the quality of the relationship, but only in terms of responsibilities and commitments. There's a sense of necessity that exists in families about maintaining those relationships, something that's above and beyond any other considerations. If I were the kind, I'd say it's something mystical. So even though it would be hard, I'd understand why she had to do it.

"They're more understanding," we say of our friends, as we ask them to stand aside while we meet the demands and obligations of family relationships. And it's true. But we pay a price for that "understanding"—a heavy cost in the kind of reciprocal commitment so many of us feel is missing from our friendships. For in asking them to understand that family comes first, we deprive our friends of the sense of entitlement that's crucial to a secure and committed relationship. And of course, we deprive ourselves as well, since we can hardly expect to get what we cannot or will not give.

3

Many Friends/Many Selves

We need friends. From early childhood on, friends help us in the lifelong process of self-development, often becoming something akin to what D. W. Winnicott has called "transitional objects"[1]—people who join us in the journey toward maturity, who facilitate our separation from the family and encourage our developing individuality by providing the contact and comfort needed for the transition from child-in-the-family to person-in-the-world.

Our friends ease the shifts and changes we experience as we live through the various life stages, sharing our experiences, our thoughts, our fears, our triumphs.[2] It is in the world of our peers that we take our measure, judge our accomplishments, whether in the internal psychological tasks of living or in the more easily observable external ones. And it is there, also, that we find support for our efforts to maintain a solid image of an adult self that is at once a unified whole while it is also made of many parts.

Unlike with kin, however, who our friends are and what kinds of relationships we have with them are dramatically affected by the turning points along the way of life. The changing panorama of our external world means also changes in our internal life which, in turn, account for the fact that so few of us carry over into adulthood old friends from childhood or adolescence.[3]

The high-school buddy who went to war instead of to college

now lives a life so different from his old friend's that there isn't much common ground anymore. The college roommates who once shared so much now see each other as virtual strangers, as one is preoccupied with career success, the other with raising two children. Even when there is some kind of continuing relationship, it rarely includes much more than an exchange of holiday or birthday greetings with notes catching each other up on the events of the year: Steve's college performance, Janet's job, Susie's surgery, Billy's wedding, Joe's layoff, Bob's promotion, the summer vacation trip.

Yet these old friends can remain significant figures in our internal lives—people to whom we made attachments, with whom we identified and who, therefore, played some part in our growth and development.[4] Consequently, people often spoke about them with some combination of pleasure in the memory and sadness about the loss.

The birthday card, the annual Christmas letter, give some reality to relationships that, in fact, have little immediate meaning on the interpersonal and interactional level. For those of us who maintain such contacts, however, they serve an important psychological function. They affirm the continuity of life; they are the living reminders of a past that memory dims unless it can be shared with another. A man who recently celebrated his seventieth birthday wept when a boyhood friend appeared at a party in his honor. Later, his daughter asked him what it meant to him, and he could only say, "He's a reminder of the boy in me." For one coming close to the end of his life, to brush up against his boyhood again is precious indeed.

Most people who see old friends from time to time complain that, like family, these friends tend to see them as they were rather than as they are becoming that, like the child who believes what he doesn't see doesn't exist, such friends resist acknowledging changes even when they are quite obvious. Speaking of these difficulties with friends from the past, a forty-year-old salesman complained:

> I have less trouble with new friends than I do with old ones because they keep wanting to put me back into some very old slots. It's like they can't see who I am now. All that's visible to them is the quiet "nebbish" I used to be, and I can't break through. So I don't see them much.

When we maintain more than such relatively inconsequential relationships with old friends, we are likely to find ourselves feeling much the same as we do with kin—the same mixture of irritation and affection as they remind us of parts of ourselves we wish to forget, as they keep trying to recall that old self by what sometimes seems to us to be their stubborn refusal to recognize the new one.

Yet the friendship survives, partly at least because its origins were grounded in some part of self and life in the past that retains meaning in the present. Therefore, there's a residue of connection and affection that remains vital and alive, along with a sense that we owe something to that shared past with whatever commitments it entailed—not just for others but for ourselves as well. A forty-nine-year-old woman, married twenty-five years, who, ten years ago, went back to a career she had set aside to raise her two children, sighed as she told of two old friends with whom she shared the earlier years of marriage and child raising:

> They're in my life, no matter what; that's all there is to it. I don't want you to think I don't care about them, because I do. But it's different with more recent friends who know me as I really am now. I've changed a lot, especially since I went back to work and have been quite successful. I feel different about myself, but I always have the feeling with these old friends that they still see the old Maggie. Except for a few people from my past like them, everyone calls me Margaret now.

In my own life, there are two such friends, women and their families who are intimately associated with my early adult years. They were my first friends in California, easing the disruption of the move from east to west. We raised our children together, shared the economic privations of those early years, fought alongside each other through the political battles that tormented the McCarthy era, laughed and cried as one over too many joys and sorrows to be counted. They sustained me and my daughter through a divorce, inviting us into their families as if we were part of them, and rejoiced in my remarriage, even though it meant I would move four hundred miles away.

With that move, however, the paths of our lives separated. They continued to live the old life in the old world; I moved into a new one. Today there are large differences between us—gaps that are not easily bridged. Yet we remain in touch, remain friends, bound together by a complex set of emotional ties that include love and obligation and a thousand moments in the past that bring meaning to the present.

We still live four hundred miles apart, but everything of consequence that happens in our lives, and much that is not, is shared. Someone dies in one family, and I fly down at once to bring what comfort I can. My daughter marries, and they fly up for the wedding, even when the time is grossly inconvenient. No lecture or media engagement, no matter how rushed, ever takes me to Los Angeles without at least a brief visit. There are other, more ordinary visits—no emergency, no special reason, just a weekend here, one there. And in between, of course, there's the telephone. All part of friendships that are perhaps not the ideal of perfection, but whose roots run deep enough to compensate for the differences between us.

Throughout our lives, friends can help to heal the wounds of the past—wounds inflicted in the family not necessarily because our kin are unkind or uncaring but because the nature of nuclear family life makes even the best family seem like a minefield of problems waiting to explode. The relative isolation of young children from other deeply loving relationships, an ideology of parental authority that repudiates physical punishment but sees nothing wrong with a show of disapproval that threatens the withdrawal of love, the absence of major figures of identification outside the immediate family constellation—all these create an intensity of need and connection that turns even the inevitable ordinary events of family life into potential problems. An older sibling leaves home and the adoring younger one feels abandoned. A new infant is brought into the family and the older child feels deprived and displaced at the very moment when parents' emotional resources are already stretched to the limit.

As we grow to adulthood, we will often unconsciously choose friends who are embodiments of these important others in our past. Sometimes the friend is a surrogate for an old love lost, for the older sister or brother who left us behind and with whom we were never again quite able to recapture the intensity of the old bond. Sometimes, when the old relationship was difficult or problematic, the chosen friend offers something different from that earlier one. In either case, friends provide the basis for a corrective emotional experience. A forty-three-year-old executive, who had behind him a lifetime of resentment of his younger brother, told of his friendship with a younger man, a surrogate brother, to whom he could give the help and affection he had so long and bitterly withheld from his sibling:

> Andy's the only man I've ever gotten close to, and I love him like a brother.

"Given what you've said about your relationship with your brother, that's an interesting metaphor," I observed. Laughing, he replied:

> Yeah, isn't it? I guess I should have said, "I love him like I never loved my brother."
>
> My wife and I did some therapy a couple of years ago when we were having a little trouble, and I began to understand then that this friendship with Andy has a lot to do with my brother. For most of my life I felt angry at my brother, and then I'd feel guilty for being angry. But after all that garbage between us, there's not

much chance of anything really good happening.

For a long time I felt like a first-class shit because I know he's got problems, and I figure at least some of them are because of me. But there's nothing I can do about it now. I tried a few years back, but it didn't work.

Andy came to work at the office about the time I began to think about all this, and I kind of glommed onto him, you might say. I've helped him find his way in the firm, paved the way for a couple of promotions, things like that. And each time I did something for him, I'd feel this funny kind of relief. But I didn't understand why I felt that way until that time in therapy. Now I know that it's like I'm making up for what I did to my brother by taking on another "little brother" and doing it right.

By giving another man what he couldn't give his brother, he relieves his guilt which, in turn, allows him to let go of his anger. For guilt is a potent fuel for keeping the flame of anger burning bright. One feeds upon the other in a powerful and vicious cycle—guilt breeding anger which generates more guilt which then engenders more anger. With this man, the internal knowledge that his anger at his infant brother was unjustified produced the guilt from which he fled with more anger.

Sometimes anger is an appropriate response to another's attempt to stimulate our guilt. When an argument between parent and child starts or ends with "After all I've done for you . . . ," the anger the child feels is a useful protection against the parent's attempt to manipulate guilt in order to gain compliance with his or her wishes. But the whole spirit of sacrifice that pervades family life and ideology is enough to generate guilt in a child, even one who is already adult, without any external stimulation.

Whether manipulated or not, guilt is one of the most difficult of all emotions for us to live with, and anger our most commonly used defense against it. Thus each follows the other as surely and as rhythmically as the tides rise and fall. In the case of the man above, his friendship with Andy helped to release him from this cycle and opened him to the more generous and giving parts of himself—qualities that had, for so long, been bound up by the rivalrous relationship with his brother. He finds himself more comfortable with who he is and how he behaves:

> I have to say, I like myself better without all that old garbage. Maybe that's what I like about Andy so much. He makes me like myself better than I have for a long time.

"He makes me like myself better"—a gift for which we turn to friends often. Assuredly we have all known people whose friendships seem to cause more trouble and pain than they cure, who choose friends who reinforce the worst rather than the best parts of themselves—the delinquent youth, the drug addict, for example. But even among such people, the friendship is likely to derive from the attempt, abortive and self-destructive though it may be, to repair the deficits of the earlier years and to shore up a wounded and fragile sense of self.

Repeatedly people spoke of the ways in which friends allow them to test out various parts of themselves, to find strengths that were perhaps hinted at earlier in their lives but were unable to find expression in the context of family relationships. A thirty-two-year-old anthropologist said:

> I didn't really know I was smart until I became friends with Myra who's a brilliant woman. I'd say something to her and she'd look impressed, like, "Wow, that's clever," and I used to be surprised. It was my friendship with her that enabled me to go back to granduate school, get my Ph.D. and become a college professor. I still have to pinch myself to make sure it's real.

We learn much about ourselves in our relationships with friends—learning that comes partly at least from who they are, how they respond to us, what we see reflected in their eyes. For friends become for us a mirror on the self; and what we see there, whether it pleasures or pains us, helps to affirm those parts of self we like and respect and to change those whose reflection brings us discomfort.

Generally, the people we call "friend" are those who seem to us to call up the best parts of ourselves, even while they also accept our darker side. A friend we think of as brilliant opens up the possibility of a new vision of our own intellectual capacities, thus pushing us beyond the limits we thought were ours. A friend who is kind, generous and especially loving elicits a like response, helping us to overcome old fears of our self-centeredness. A thirty-eight-year-old personnel manager who talked at length about her impoverished relationship with her mother also told of the importance in her life of her closest friend, a woman eighteen years older than she. Her mother, she said, had filled her ears with recriminations about how difficult she was, with repeated charges that she was a spoiled, selfish child.

> For years I was convinced nobody could really love me. After all, if your own mother tells you how unlovable you are, what can you expect from anyone else? But my friendship with Cynthia has really helped to change that. It's like a healing salve on an old wound to be with her.
>
> It's no secret to either of us that one of the important things I get in my friendship with her is the kind of loving mothering I never really had. We've been intimate friends for more than ten years and every minute has been precious to me—to her too, I'm sure, but we're talking about me now. For me, this friendship has provided the place to combat the selfish brat image that I grew up with. That's how my mother saw me—still sees me, in fact. Can you imagine what a relief it was for me to find out that I can really be a loving and generous person? [*Tears springing to her eyes*] I swear I didn't know it for years.

A few weeks later I talked with Cynthia, who, at fifty-six, told of finding in her relationship with Betsy the daughter who died at the age of nine some twenty-four years earlier.

I suppose there's nothing in this life that's worse than losing a child to death. There's no way to make sense out of it, and it took my husband and me a long time to be able to live normally again. We have another child, a son, and he's wonderful. But I've always yearned for that little girl who died before she had a chance to live.

When I met Betsy—it's ten or eleven years ago now—something about her tugged at my heart the way nothing had for too many years. So she became the daughter I wanted so badly, and I could lavish love on her because she needed that as badly as I needed a girl to give it to.

It's like something broke open inside me for the first time in all those years. We talk about what we mean to each other, of course, and we're both aware of what a wonderful gift we've given each other. In some ways, she's given me back a zest for life that I was never quite able to recapture until I met her. Oh, I don't mean I didn't live a full life; I did. It's something very subtle I'm talking about, maybe something like draining an old abscess finally.

Friends help also to affirm new roles undertaken, parts of self not formerly met. A man becomes a husband and befriends other men who share his new role, thus affirming the shift from single to married and helping to give it an internal reality. We leave behind the role of student and enter the professional world, only to find we wear the new title uneasily, as if it doesn't quite fit, especially if we have in any way exceeded the expectations with which we were raised. A forty-one-year-old woman told how, when she first became a doctor, she turned to friends to make more real this part of herself she had not yet fully internalized.

When I was finishing medical school, and even for the first couple of years of my residency, I had this feeling that nobody would ever believe I was a real doctor. I suppose that's because I didn't really believe it either. It was important for me then to be friends with other physicians, especially other women physicians, because we talked about how it all felt unreal, and could support and validate each other.

Sometimes we choose a friend who mirrors our fantasies, dreams of a self we wish we could be. A man who lives a life of constraint tells of the relief and excitement he feels in the presence of a friend who "lives very close to his impulses."

> In a way, my friend Bob is the kind of person I'd like to be. I don't mean I want to do exactly what he does. He drinks a lot and screws a lot, things like that. He lives right on the edge all the time. I don't want to be as excessive as he is, but I think about how much lighter I'd feel to live a little more in his style. When I'm with him, I can get a little closer to being less controlled and uptight; it's like he brings out that part of me.

Such friendships, of course, may do nothing more than permit us to live vicariously through them. But the choice of these friends, seemingly so different from ourselves, may also signal the emergence of a part of the self that had hitherto been hidden from view. For we are all more complex, with more varied traits and potentialities, than we know and can see. In all of us, parts of the self have been subordinated—sometimes perhaps to the more dominant parts of our personality, sometimes to those to which we could more safely give expression in the earlier years of life, sometimes in conformity with the cultural commandments of our times, often some combination of all of the above.

A new friend, then, one who is different from us or from others in our life, is not the result of some random event or accidental meeting. Rather, this may be the first sign that we are ready to drop the defenses that have inhibited the expression of some part of self, the first glimmering that some part not yet consciously known is ready to emerge or, in more extreme cases, the first public expression of what Winnicott has called the "true self" that has been hidden under the "false self" usually on display.[5]

About this true self–false self dichotomy, however, there is much yet to be said. Although useful as a metaphor for conceptualizing certain problems of the self seen in the clinical setting, it is, I believe, too sharply drawn and, therefore, usually too rigidly interpreted to render adequately the complexities of this entity we call a "self."

In reality, *I am convinced there is no one true self or false self. Instead, the true self can be seen as an integration of the various parts of self of which I have been speaking here—an integration that is more or less complete, but never wholly so at any given era in the history of a life.* For there probably are parts of self that are always in the process of becoming—parts that develop in response to a passage under way, to a new role undertaken, to a crisis that calls upon strengths never before encountered.

Just so, except in cases of extreme pathology, we rarely see a wholly false self. Winnicott argues that the false self is not just an external public face presented to the world; it becomes the internal private one as well, the true self being buried so deeply as to become inaccessible.

Certainly I have no wish to quarrel with the notion that the surroundings within which we live and grow play a crucial part in our development. I am also firmly committed to the belief that how we are expected to act defines not only our behavior but, in profoundly important ways, our sense of our self. The problem with Winnicott's formulation, however, as with those of other theorists of this persuasion, is that the family, and in particular the mother-infant dyad, is the *only* social environment credited with a significant part in the developmental script. Later years, different experiences, other people—all are seen as ancillary to the main event, not affecting who we are, what we become, how we live and relate to others, in any serious and consistent way.

Without dismissing or diminishing the significance of the early childhood years in the family, my own view encompasses a much wider base. My argument is that there is no single set of relationships, no single social institution, that can determine so completely the future of our psychological development. For just as there is no single unitary entity called "society" that, except at the broadest levels, determines who we are and how we will act, so there is no unitary entity called a "self," whether a true self or a false one. Instead, the various microsocieties within which we live from childhood on—the family, the park playground, the neighborhood, the schoolroom, the social club, the teen-age peer group, the church, the place where we work—all play their part in our formation, all call upon the self in its various and different capacities, all require us to display some part of self, to withhold another.

Without doubt, in those situations where a person sees compliance with external demands as necessary to psychological survival, those parts of self that are called into question will be hidden from view. But there is also no doubt that, except in the extreme case, we are speaking of *parts* of the self, not the whole of it, and that other parts will continue to be seen, heard and experienced.

This conception of the self as a shifting amalgam of the various and complex facets that make up an individual permits us to understand more readily how it is that a person can seem at once so competent and in control about some things and so much the opposite about others, so well-developed in some areas and so ill-developed in others. The woman who confidently goes about the task of mothering and homemaking while appearing wholly uncertain about her capacities in the world outside this sphere is a good example.

We have all seen such people, found ourselves puzzled about them and the way their sense of themselves seems to shift and change. In the clinical setting we tend to think of this as a problem of pathology—at best, the inability to present the "true self" to both self and other; at worst, the problem of a fragmented self.

Although these interpretations can sometimes be useful, I believe they also blind us to the intricacies of the self and its development, often sending us and our patients searching in vain for a single core of self that does not exist. Instead, the whole issue of the self is better understood as a dynamic and ongoing process of development in which various parts of self are more or less accessible to us, depending upon the historical moment in a life, upon the roles we are called upon to play and, most important in the context of this discussion, upon the friends who people our lives.

In this matter of friends, there's little evidence to support the claim of psychoanalytically oriented theorists that the strength or weakness of a person's adult relationships can be traced *directly* to the early experiences in the family.[6] Indeed, their almost exclusive preoccupation with relations in the family during the first few years of life has blinded even the most advanced psychoanalytic thinkers to the logical implications of their own theories.[7] For if, as most now agree, the human infant develops a sense of self and identity through the internalization of people and things from the external world, why would that not be a process that continues through life? Why would only mother, father, sister, brother count? Why not friends as well?

As research into adult development has flourished, there is more and more evidence that we are more malleable and more adaptable than psychoanalytically oriented theories have suggested, that later years and other events make their mark, that even objectively difficult childhood experiences will, more than likely, affect some of us differently than others.[8] But the current debate among these students of human development about whether we can leave those first years behind or not misses the mark.

The issue, it seems to me, is not whether there's continuity in human development from birth to death. Of course there is. Nor is it whether discontinuity exists. Certainly it does. Both exist in a continuing tension in all of us as we strive to maintain a coherent and stable sense of self while, at the same time, we continue to find previously unknown parts of ourselves as we integrate new experiences, new roles, new people into our lives. These two threads in human life—continuity and discontinuity—ought not be seen as opposing each other; rather the theorists who argue for one side or the other come to their research looking for different things, therefore see a different set of facts.

In the research for this book, for example, I met people whose early lives were racked with the agony of loneliness and isolation both inside the family and out, yet who now have a rich and varied network of friends. The theorists who argue for discontinuity and change as the dominant experience in human development would find in this a confirmation of their views. And in some ways, they would be right. But psychoanalytically oriented observers, looking at the same external behavior, would want to know what internal meaning it had for the person, how the earlier experience was processed, how it fit into this new one. In that examination, they would most likely see, as I did, that inside the adult who now seems so comfortable in the social world lives the child who was always on the edge of the crowd, who lived life at the margins rather than at its center. Therefore, the adult often continues to *feel* different or marginal even when it is clearly no longer the case.

So, for example, a personable, attractive and very successful forty-one-year-old businessman who told of his lonely youth lives today in a wide circle of social relationships, if not intimate friends. Yet his internal sense of himself and his life is still dominated by the childhood experience. He's not unaware of the discrepancy between his internal experience and the external reality; nevertheless, the feelings persist.

> I know it doesn't make sense given what my life is like. But hell, I don't ever fully get rid of feeling like I'm not really part of it all,

> like I'm just a little bit off from where everybody else is, you know, like I don't *really* belong.

Some people make their peace with such an internal sense of marginality by cultivating a marginal life style with friends who feel equally on the fringe, then defining their small world as the more desirable one than the mainstream way of life. Such people are not necessarily unaware of the choices they have made. They make no claim to being anything but marginal, indeed insist that they have no wish to be, that theirs is the more enviable life. But while the choice itself may be in conscious awareness, the *reasons* for it, and the self-doubt and conflict such a defense usually is designed to obscure, may well be hidden from the view of both the individual and the observer whose research tools do not permit the kind of depth examination necessary to ferret them out.

The psychoanalysts are not unaware of the actual life changes such people make; nor do they wholly fail to credit their importance. But they also argue for the need to understand and change the inner psychic structure to match the external behavior. Only then will a new sense of self be freed to come to the fore, they say; only then can we be certain that the behavioral changes will remain in place. With this as their concern, they look to the internal life of the individual to answer their questions about change and stability and, in cases such as these, come down on the side of continuity.

Looking at the same people, other developmental theorists will argue that they present us with a clear demonstration of change and discontinuity over the course of a life. It's not that these researchers are wholly unconcerned about the inner life. Rather their dominant interest lies in the observable ways people manage their external lives, how they resolve problems from the past irrespective of how they *feel* about them or themselves while doing so.

Neither is wholly right, neither completely wrong. The theoretical views they bring to their task define the tools with which they work, the questions they ask, and how they assess the answers they hear. Consequently, they are able to illuminate only one part of human life and development.

To me, it seems unquestionable that the hurts and deprivations of early life do not *entirely* disappear from the inner psychic life, no matter what changes we may make, either in the external environment or in the internal one. Nor is their impact negligible to our developing sense of self. But if the events of later life did not have any corrective potential, then all of us who are clinicians might as well pack up our tools and go home. For whatever else it might accomplish by way of insight and understanding, the central task of the therapeutic interaction is to provide an experience that will heal.

Since a self develops out of our experiences in the world, out of the many ways we see ourselves mirrored in the eyes of others, out of the ways we internalize and integrate those experiences at different times in our lives, it's reasonable to assume that there are many selves that live inside us. It's time, therefore, for a new metaphor to symbolize the analytic process.

Until now, the idea has been that psychoanalysis is like peeling an onion, layer after layer gently removed until the real core of self stands revealed. A more appropriate image, it seems to me, is the tapestry—a cloth woven together of a variety of different threads, each blending into the whole while also recognizable as a distinct and separate part.[9] And as with a tapestry, damage to the self can be repaired with the right "thread." From a distance, the repair is not noticeable; up close it becomes visible once again.

As adults, most people find a place among friends in their lives, a place where, as they said frequently in one way or another, they can believe they count, where they can be accepted for the qualities in themselves they hold dear, can be validated for those they hope to develop. Through these relationships with friends, the pain of the past has been softened, sometimes even healed. The healing leaves scars, of course—scars that can be irritated, even if not fully opened, when a new experience replays an old one. But each positive experience with a new friend brings with it the courage and confidence to take the next step, to develop a new part of self, a different view of some of the old parts. It isn't a quick or easy process; it goes on for years. But through it, we find our way to new beginnings, new ways of seeing ourselves and new ways of being in the world.

With such a conception of the self we can make sense of the kinds of changes we have all experienced in our own lives—changes that often seem magical to us, so out of consciousness are they when they're in process. A person who has all the outward signs of the ebullient extrovert forms a close friendship with a quiet, reflective introvert and expresses surprise: "It's so uncharacteristic of me to be friends with someone like that." Yet as the friendship develops, she or he takes on some of the friend's coloration, finding the quieter side of self, appreciating more intensely the time spent alone.

I know the experience well, having watched in wonder this very shift in my own life. After years of childhood and adolescent loneliness, in adulthood I finally had the life filled with friends for which I had hungered. Even my work as a political organizer and manager of political campaigns kept me surrounded with people I liked and respected, feelings that clearly were shared. Whatever worries remained about whether I could have friends, whether people could care about me, were constantly reassured. Now my problem was only how I could see all those who had some claim on my time and energy.

Then suddenly, as if not of my own will, it all changed when, in my late thirties, I decided to go to school for the college education I didn't yet have. For the first time, I touched the part of me that today looks toward the isolation of writing as one hungers for food after a fast.

It's only now, as I look back, that I can see the seeds of that change already present in my friendship choices toward the end of the earlier period of my life. Until then, my friends came almost entirely from the political world in which I lived and worked. But I was beginning to experience some inchoate yearnings for something else, although I didn't know what. I knew only that I felt somewhat disenchanted with the work, somewhat restless with my friends.

It was then that I met and became fast friends with a woman who also had been a political activist but who was, when we met, a graduate student—a woman who read books and spoke of ideas I'd not yet heard of, who seemed to me the smartest person I'd ever known. Yet she wanted to be my friend as much as I wanted to be hers, making it possible for me to begin to believe that I, too, might be smart, even that I could do what she had done.

Within two years, I was a student, and the shift to some new equilibrium between the extrovert-introvert parts of myself was under way. Having reassured the anxieties about the public self, I was able then to turn my attention to the further development of the private one.

It's not just for affirmation of those as yet unrealized parts of self that we look to friends, however. They also affirm and reflect back to us parts of ourselves that, although fully formed, are not in conformity with the norms to which we were socialized. A fifty-five-year-old woman, for example, told how friends were important to an identity that was not commonly accepted in the earlier years of her life.

> I've always been a jock, long before it was fashionable for women to be running around in exercise suits. But for most of my life it wasn't easy to find athletic women, and I was somewhat self-conscious about it. I never did give it up, though, and I was always looking for friends to do athletic things with. Like I said, they

were hard to find, so when I found them, they were like a treasure.

"Was it just the company you wanted in those years, or was there something else you were looking for as well?" I asked. She looked at me puzzled for a moment, then, with a smile of comprehension:

Oh, I know what you mean. Sure there was something else. I didn't want to feel like a freak.

The assurance that she's not "a freak," the yearning for belonging the words imply, is comfort that friends can give when family cannot. The very lack of choice that defines kin relations makes their reassurances about ourselves and our worth suspect. A mother tells a daughter who feels ugly that she's beautiful, and the child thinks to herself, "Sure, she's my mother; what else can she say?" Parents reassure an offspring who doubts one or another of his or her capabilities, and the child thinks, "What do they know?"

Every psychotherapist has listened to any number of agonized tales from adults about how their parents' constant reassurances fell on deaf ears and impenetrable psyches. Sometimes the children are right in their doubts. Some parents may, in fact, be unable to perceive or judge a child's capacities objectively. Others may be under the false impression that it is helpful to reassure a child regardless of the reality. In either case, the false assurances make it difficult both to believe the parents and to integrate a sense of self that's grounded in reality. But even when parents are able and willing to respond to the child's sense of self-in-the-world in ways that match her or his experience, the doubts will remain if they are not assuaged by peers who demonstrate their respect and approval by choosing to become a friend.

The wish not "to feel like a freak," the need to belong as an affirmation of self and identity, is a principal force motivating all who band together in what we might think of as outlaw communities—that is, communities of people who, by virtue of their race, ethnicity, sexual identity or gender, share what Erving Goffman has called "a spoiled identity."[10] Gay pride, Black pride, Arab pride, Jewish pride, Italian pride, Irish pride—it's all the same for any group anywhere whose people have felt the lash of prejudice and discrimination. All would understand these words from a thirty-four-year-old lesbian, out of the closet for over a decade, who must still defend her lesbian identity against a variety of threats:

> It's very important to have friends who you know are like you, especially if you live in a world that doesn't much value what you are. So from the first, my lesbian friends were terribly important to me. There's a sense with them of sharing something that's distinctively ours and that makes us special in a way that nobody outside the lesbian community can understand.
>
> That's what makes it so hard if someone you're close to decides to go straight. It happened to me recently with someone I love and respect a lot. She's a very neat, wonderful person, and the fact that this great woman was gay reflected on me as a gay person. I could bask in her light. I don't know if you can understand what I mean, but for me, it was like the seal of approval of my own gayness. It made me proud to be a lesbian because I knew I was like her. So when she ended up going straight, it was a terrible shock to me. It shook me up in my own sense of myself and my lesbianism for a while.

For blacks, the person who passes; for Jews, the one who converts—these send the same kind of shock waves through the psyche, telegraph a similar message about the cost of a socially devalued identity. It's true for members of marginal political groups as well. The special bonding that comes from being joined in dissent, of feeling outside the mainstream, is central in the maintenance of self and identity among the members. As one forty-two-year-old man, an activist of the political left, said:

> Being an outsider—I mean, being a dissenter politically—is a very important impetus for developing very close, tight bonds with people who share the experience. The shared status in itself creates a kind of identification that brings people close. When you feel yourself marked off from the world around you, you absolutely need that kind of closeness with similar people. That sense of belonging to a very different kind of fraternal order, where you share a set of values and beliefs that sets you apart in a positive way, is one of the highs of the movement. It's a good part of what holds people and keeps them committed.

When, for whatever reason, values change and allegiances shift, the reaction of those who are left behind is intense—experienced as a threat both to the group and to all its adherents hold dear. In the old Communist party, for example, the women and men who left became non-persons—unseen when they were clearly in view, unheard when they spoke plainly within earshot. In theory, they were dealt with so harshly because they were considered traitors to the cause and a danger to those who remained. But the emotional and symbolic significance of the behavior was, I believe, more important. For in joining in the common revulsion against the defectors, the members affirmed their unity, their identity and their uniqueness, giving each other "the seal of approval" of which the lesbian above spoke so eloquently.

For all of us, by permitting us to see ourselves in the mirror of their affection, friends help to anchor our self-image, to validate our identity. For those who live outside the pale, this is doubly important—the central motivation for the tendency to band together in friendships among themselves. Whether it is color, class, ethnic background or sexual identity that is the basis for the prejudice directed toward them, friendships with others like self became crucial in fortifying and maintaining self-esteem. A twenty-eight-year-old black man who works in an almost entirely white environment talked of the prejudices he hears every day and the pain it causes him:

> I get enough of the damn white world and their stinking racism every day. I'm glad to come home where I don't have to hear anyone complain about "lazy spades" or watch them swallow the word "nigger" when they notice me, and crap like that. What do you think it makes *me* feel like? So you ask me if I have white friends? Well, let me tell you, when I want to feel okay, I stick with my own.

Not much different, is it, from the twenty-six-year-old homosexual who talked about the difficulties of coping with the negative response from the straight world that surrounds him?

> Most of my friends are gay now because I can't be myself with straight people, even when they know I'm gay. I mean, being gay influences my whole life; there's no question about it. How do I say it? It affects how I look at politics, at sex, just about everything. Let's say I'm walking down the street with some men from the office and they see a pretty girl. That's all they talk about; you know, all the things men say: "Look at that." "What a piece of ass." But if I see some cute guy who turns me on, can I say the same things about him? You better bet your sweets I can't. Christ, I'm not interested in their ogling girls any more than they get off on my thing with guys. But I *have* to listen to their shit if I'm with them because they're the "normal" ones, and I'd just be another goddamned faggot if I opened up and said what I was thinking.

It is true, of course, that such intense concern with one part of identity can be narrow and restrictive, inhibiting the full and varied growth of other parts of self that a wider range of friends would encourage. Several men and women spoke about the way their life among gay friends sometimes feels confining, about the fact that other facets of self tend to be put on hold as they struggle to maintain a gay identity. But it is almost inevitable that, when one central part of identity is stigmatized, it begins to transcend other aspects of the self, becoming central precisely because it is the part that must be defended.

About gays, the straight world complains, "Why do they have

to make such a fuss? Who cares whom they sleep with?" But the truth is that we do care, and "they" now make "a fuss" precisely because so many forces in our society conspire to disconfirm them, because the invisibility that was formerly their lot in itself nullifies a part of self that, like a heterosexual identity, deserves to be seen and honored.

Only when the designations "gay" and "straight" are seen by the heterosexual world as equally legitimate expressions of sexual preference will being gay become a less salient personal characteristic for all of us, whether we're gay or straight. Only then will most gay people be able to believe that, as one man said, "there's a life after gay."

Throughout our lives, then, we have friends and "just" friends, old friends and new friends, good friends and best friends—each relationship meeting some part of ourselves that cries out for expression. One friend taps our intellectual capacities more deeply than others, another connects most profoundly to our emotional side. One calls upon our nurturant, caretaking qualities, another permits our dependency needs to surface. One friend touches our fun-loving side, another our more serious part. One friend is the sister we wish we had, another offers the mothering we missed.

The depth of a friendship—how much it means to us, whether we say we're "friends" or "best friends"—depends, at least in part, upon how many parts of ourselves a friend sees, shares and validates. For what a friend sees and reflects back to us is at once important in affirming and validating the various parts of self as well as the whole gestalt we call a self. Speaking about the range of possible friendships, a fifty-three-year-old woman gave voice to the fantasy of a peerless friend with whom all parts of self could be shared.

> At the ideal end of the spectrum would be the friend who knows and can value all parts of you. What I mean is, supposing you have ten parts to yourself. With most people you can interact and share

> maybe one or two of them. Sometimes you get lucky and you can share more than that. And once or twice in a whole lifetime maybe, with real luck, you find someone you can share all of your ten parts with. Then you only have to hope that, as any of those parts change in yourself, they'll continue to mesh with the other person. Or, if you're luckiest of all, you'll both keep changing and growing in the same direction. That's asking a lot, maybe too much, isn't it?

Perhaps only with an identical twin is this not "asking a lot, maybe too much." Interestingly, I happened upon some identical twins in the course of this study, all of whom saw their twin as just this kind of mirror of self.[11] All took comfort in having what one woman described as "someone who's so much like you, you only have to look at her to know what you think and feel." But unlike most of us who long to find another like self, for twins, who even as adults can't be told apart except by those closest to them, there has been too much likeness. For them, the need to feel different, to experience their separate identity more keenly, dominates their search for friends.

> I feel sort of overdone in the "like me" category, having been a twin. So the friends I'm closest to are different. I'm short and dark and have a fiery temperament, and they're all tall and thin and not nearly as demonstrative and emotional. I love the differences between us. It's a relief for me to be with them and to know I'm different and admired for that. It means I have my own place in the world.

For the rest of us, whose "place in the world" sometimes feels too separate, it can be hard to give up the yearning for the kind of likeness that twins find so difficult. Our search for the perfect friend, lover or mate rests on the dream that somewhere there's another just like self, that sometime we will be able to recreate that brief period of our infancy when we felt ourselves to be one with our mother, when faultless communion with another seemed possible. We want someone to know us in just this deep and intimate way—someone who mirrors our own feelings perfectly because of feeling the same way, someone who values all the various parts of ourselves even when they are not shared.

Yet as I have indicated, not all friendships require this kind of loving unity to serve us well and satisfy our needs. The friend who meets a particular part in us, the one who crosses our life for a brief moment at a crucial developmental point—these all have their place. A woman who heard I was writing about friendship wrote me to say, among other things: "We can't live our lives only experiencing the deeper emotions; there has to be room (and relief) for the lighter ones. Sometimes a conversation with a more casual friend can be like a light repast as compared to the heavier meal of deep involvement with my intimate friend."

Indeed, this is one of the gifts of friendship that's not easily found in other intimate relationships, with their emphasis on exclusivity. Certainly in friendships there are jealousies, possessiveness and the wish for exclusive rights and privileged access. But in neither our internal world nor the external one are such wishes accorded the legitimacy they get in a marriage or love relationship. Among friends, therefore, many friends are possible to meet the many selves that live inside us.

4

Men, Women and Friends

The Differences Between Us

For as long as the word has been written, men's friendships have been taken to be the model of what friendship is and how it ought to be. From the Greek philosophers to modern writers like Lionel Tiger,[1] major treatises have been devoted to friendship among men—to the depth of their bonding, the intensity of their love, their enduring commitment. Men, it has been written, give each other comfort, support, validation, love—even fulfillment and completion, the very wholeness that, in modern times, is the preserve of lovers. In his essay "On Friendship," Sir Francis Bacon wrote that without a friend, men were "as an half piece," that they needed "a friend to make it entire," that they might be "princes that had wives, sons, nephews; and yet all these could not supply the comfort of friendship."[2]

But friendship was for men only. Only men, wrote Jeremy Taylor in his *Discourse on Friendship,* were "capable of all those excellencies by which men can oblige the world"[3]—and of course, each other. Women's friendships didn't count, indeed were not even noticed. For just as women have been invisible in public life throughout the ages, so their private relations with each other have been unseen as well. Thus long before Sigmund Freud turned the historic male prejudices about women into a theory about their ill-developed superego, women were considered to be too childlike, too given to instability, to petty jealousies and trivial concerns, to be able to maintain friendships.

It took the present-day feminist historians to set the record straight. In a pioneering article, Carroll Smith-Rosenberg wrote: "The female friendship of the nineteenth century, the long-lived, intimate, loving friendship between two women, is an excellent example of the type of historical phenomena which most historians know something about, which few have thought much about, and which virtually no one has written about. It is one aspect of the female experience which consciously or unconsciously we have chosen to ignore."[4]

As we move closer to the present, the romantic and impassioned descriptions of men's friendships that were so much a part of the literature of earlier eras disappear almost entirely from view. Now, instead of lyrical tributes to the glory of male friendships, we have laments about men's problems with intimacy and vulnerability, about the impoverishment of their relationships with each other—at least among heterosexual men.[5] Now we have Leonard Michaels's portrayal of modern men in ordinary circumstances—a pungent and devastating tale of men in a desperate, yet doomed, search for connection with others like themselves.[6] Now, almost as a postscript to his book on male development, Daniel Levinson tells us that, in the many hours he spent interviewing each man in his study, "friendship was largely noticeable by its absence."[7] Now *Newsweek* magazine publishes a commentary about the paucity of close and nurturing relations among men in which the author writes with sadness and envy: "I've always been amazed at the nurturing emotional support that my wife can seek and return with her close female friends. Often the most intimate and intense problems are shared and therefore diminished through empathy. Her three-hour talks with friends refresh and renew her far more than my three-mile jogs restore me. In our society it seems as if you've got to have a bosom to be a buddy."[8]

The results of my own research are unequivocal: At every life stage between twenty-five and fifty-five, women have more friendships, as distinct from collegial relationships or workmates, than men, and the differences in the content and quality of their friendships are marked and unmistakable.[9]

Other research shows that these differences persist right up through old age, as women continue to make new friends while men lose old ones without replacement.[10] It's true that some studies show men reporting larger numbers of friends than women do.[11] But this has more to do with men's propensity for naming as a friend anyone with whom they have some ongoing association—co-workers, neighbors, tennis partners, members of the bowling team—while women tend to use the term "friend" more selectively.

Generally, women's friendships with each other rest on shared intimacies, self-revelation, nurturance and emotional support.[12] A forty-six-year-old secretary, married twenty-five years, said:

> There are a lot of people I can play with, but the people I call my real friends are the ones I can talk to also. I mean, they're the people I can share *myself* with, not just my time.

In contrast, men's relationships are marked by shared activities.[13] What they do may differ by age and class, but that they tend to *do* rather than *be* together is undeniable. Thus a twenty-eight-year-old worker in an oil refinery, married and the father of two children, said:

> We go to the pool hall and shoot pool, maybe hit a bar or two and drink and tell stories and all that kind of stuff—just raise a little hell.

"What counts as raising hell?" I wanted to know.

> I don't know. Maybe drink a little more than we should and take the trucks out and run them up and down the hills around here. Make a lot of noise, things like that.

And a professional man of about the same age, also married, with one small child, said:

> I play tennis with one of my friends every week. Every now and then I'll go to a ball game with a couple of friends, or we'll get

> together to watch some big game on the tube. Since the baby was born, it's hard for Susan and me to get out together a lot, so sometimes I'll go to a movie with a friend.

Talk usually centers around work, sports, sharing expertise, whether about how to fix a leak in the roof or about which of the new wine releases are worthy of cellaring. And of course, they trade complaints and concerns about women, along with tales of exploits. But most of the time, their interactions are emotionally contained and controlled, a fact that occasioned comment from a few of the men. A thirty-nine-year-old city planner put it this way:

> The men I know, including myself, operate more on abstracted images than on underlying feelings. If you listen in on any conversation between two men, that's what you'll hear from them—the kind of talk that's always general and abstract, not about themselves and things that are personal.

"Do you have a best friend?" I asked all the men and women I met.

Over three-fourths of the single women had no problem in identifying a best friend, and almost always that person was a woman. Among those who had no one who fit the bill, only very few failed to speak spontaneously about how they regret not having someone to whom they felt close enough to say they were best friends.

"I haven't had anyone that close to me since Sue moved away, and I miss it."

"I have some very good friends, but no one I can call a best friend right now. But I'm looking."

"From the time I was a kid, I almost always had a best friend. But since I moved to Washington, there's no one. This is a tough town for that kind of really intimate friendship, maybe because people are always moving in and out of it."

"There's a big empty space where Nora used to live, and it'll take time to fill it."

In sharp contrast to the women, over two-thirds of the single men could not name a best friend. Equally interesting, this was not something that seemed troubling to most of them. Some few men, of course, spoke thoughtfully, even with some concern, feeling there was something lacking in their lives, something they were helpless to change. A thirty-four-year-old architect said:

> No, no one I know is in that standout category of best friend that you had when you were in high school or college. I sometimes wonder about it, and I guess I even wish it were different. It would be nice. But it doesn't seem to happen when you're a busy adult.

But most tended to shrug the question off casually, as if, as one man said, "Best friends are for kids." Another man, apparently piqued by our discussion, flung out, "Only a woman would have so damn many questions about friends and make it so important."

Of the single men who were able to name a best friend, it was much more likely to be a woman than a man who held that place in their lives. Some couldn't explain why, insisting that it was just happenstance, an accident that had no particular meaning.

"It's just one of those things, no reason for it."

"It's no big deal. We just like each other best, that's all."

But most of the men who claimed a woman as a best friend talked about the difficulties of establishing close relations with men.

"I get along better with women because I can be more open with a woman."

"I've tried reaching out to men from time to time, but they don't reciprocate, and I begin to feel like the friendship stands or falls on my initiative. Then I feel rejected, and it's harder to bounce back from that with a man than a woman. Nobody likes to feel they've been vulnerable to another man."

"Women have a special way of being friends. They're more

emotionally open and expressive than men."

"I think men are afraid of each other. It's like we've been trained to be on guard."

"I can be more spontaneous with a woman. When I'm with a man I watch myself—you know, guard the flank."

Such fears and feelings are not, of course, given to single men alone. It's common gossip among professional women, for example, that while their male colleagues, married or single, will exchange professional talk with each other, when they want a sympathetic ear for their problems they invite a woman to lunch. But except for such work-based relationships, married men usually don't have women friends outside the framework of marriage. Therefore, they are even less likely than single men to have a best friend. When they named anyone at all, it was most often a wife.

"The problem is time; I don't have time for friends"—the explanation I heard most frequently from men who are married. It isn't that they don't want to see friends, don't value these relationships, they insisted, but by the time the workday is done and the family attended to, there's little time or energy left for friends.

"I don't have time"—a lament that's commonplace in the life of any adult. For time is a familiar enemy, one most of us fight against in a battle we seem destined to lose. I wondered, therefore, if, among women who work at full-time jobs, close friendships also are sacrificed to time. They, too, complain about time, about the pressures they feel as they try to meet the responsibilities of work and family.

"I'm always fighting the clock."

"Before I know it, it's eleven o'clock and I'm dead tired. All I can do is fall into bed."

"Time, time, time. If I could have anything I asked for, it would be a few more hours in every day."

"There's never enough time to do what I have to do right. I always feel like I don't put enough time in anywhere, not at work or at home."

Yet even working women who are also raising young children and tending a household usually manage at least one or two important friendships. Therefore, it was no problem for most of these women to name at least one close friend who was not also a mate. Indeed, whether they worked outside the home or not, few women thought of a husband in these terms, not because there were no shared intimacies between them, not because the relationship wasn't close and important, but because the women usually had friends with whom they shared parts of themselves as well. Therefore, they made clear distinctions between a friend and a mate in ways the men did not. As a forty-two-year-old woman, married eighteen years and a part-time real estate broker, said:

> Andy says I'm his best friend, and sometimes I feel bad because I don't say the same about him. But I really think the only reason he says it is because he doesn't have any friends himself. He never has had any since we got married.
>
> I don't mean that I don't love him and feel very close to him. I do. But it's different than my relationship with Ginny and what I feel for her. My life is tied to Andy's, so our relationship is very complex and it has a lot of layers. But a best friend, well, that's something else. I go to her for a different kind of sharing and comfort and understanding.

"How do you maintain close friendships when work and family take up so much of your time?" I asked all the women who talked about the time pressures in their lives. As if speaking with one voice, they agreed it was hard, agreed it was an added weight in an already overburdened life. "Why do you do it, then?" I wondered. Most were perplexed by the question, wondering what to say about something that seemed so self-evident to them:

"I almost don't know what to say. I have to, that's all."

"What can I say, my friends are very important to me."

"Am I crazy or something, or would other people feel like I do right now—like you asked me why I get up in the morning?"

"I love my husband and my kids, but they can't give me what I get from my women friends. I need them in my life too."

"I need them in my life too"—words spoken easily by a woman, though rare indeed to hear anything faintly resembling such sentiments from a man. The difference is not in the amount of time available but in what an intimate relationship with someone of the same sex means to each of them.

Women *make* time for such friendships because they value them so highly, because they offer a shared intimacy that's quite different from what they experience in a relationship with a man. But given the wariness with which men approach each other, given their fear of displaying vulnerability or dependency to another man, there's not much incentive to find time for friends who are more than playmates.

Even when a man spoke of a best friend, the two usually shared little about the interior of their lives and feelings. Men who claimed years of close friendship failed to confide to each other their distress at any number of conflicts, especially those that touched their personal or work lives in ways they feared would diminish their stature.

One man didn't tell his best friend he had been fired until it was no longer possible to keep the secret; another didn't speak to anyone but his wife when a promised promotion failed to materialize. A man who had been laid off because of a plant closing told how he stayed home for months rather than bear the humiliation of seeing friends who were still working. And it wasn't unusual to hear a man say he didn't know a friend's marriage was in serious trouble until the man appeared on his doorstep asking if he could sleep on the couch.

These men talked with each other about work, women and marriage, of course. They spoke about problems on the job; they joked about marriage and its hardships; they shared their views about the differences between women and men, about the difficulty in understanding "them." But it was an abstract discussion, held under cover of an intellectual search for understanding rather than a revelation of their lives and feelings. They didn't say to each other, "Promotions are due and I'm worried I'll be passed over." "My wife is talking about leaving me and I don't know what to do to keep her." Instead, a thirty-two-year-old accountant, married six years, said, when I asked if he talked to his "good friends" about problems and conflicts in his family:

> Yeah, sure. But you don't just come right out and say it straight. You do it by sort of telling a story or saying something about women in general—something like that. So you get it off your chest, and you listen to what they have to say and get some other ideas about how to handle the problem. It's like confiding in them without actually telling them anything up front. I mean, it's all very general and you don't let on you're really talking about yourself and your wife.

One of the men I spoke with, a twenty-seven-year-old construction worker, told me about an affair his wife had had three years earlier that nearly wrecked their marriage. Since he was one of the few men I met who had a genuinely close and loving relationship with another man, I asked if he had discussed the situation with his friend.

"Did you talk to Steve about how you were feeling or what you might do?"

"No, of course not," he answered.

"Why do you say 'of course'? I would have expected that you'd talk to your closest friend about something that was so upsetting to you."

With his head bent so he wouldn't have to look at me, "Well, I wouldn't."

"I'm really trying to understand. Could you try to tell me why not?"

A moment of silence, then, with a wave of a hand as if to dismiss the subject, "It's just not something I could talk about, that's all. Hell, I don't know. I was hurt and ashamed and angry, and I felt like crying and like killing her and the son-of-a-bitch who got her involved, who was a guy I knew. How could I tell anybody all that?"

"You just told me, and I'm a stranger."

"That's different. You're a woman; it's easier to talk to a woman." Then, with an impish grin, "Besides, what do I care what you think? You'll walk out of here and I'll never see you again, but my friends . . . I have to live with them."

When asked to explain their failure to speak of more personal matters with their friends, many men, both single and married, were quick to acknowledge that they couldn't share the pain they felt, couldn't risk allowing another man to see their vulnerability. Some of the married men, however, credited an inbred sense of privacy, a deep-seated belief that marriage requires that kind of loyalty. Good reasons—reasons to be honored. But when pushed, most of them also acknowledged that they didn't talk to friends about the fears and conflicts inside them that have nothing to do with anyone else—about their disappointments in themselves, about their fear of failure, about the difficulty of always having to put on a show of strength and independence.

What does this say about the quality of the emotional tie between men? Are we to understand from all this that men have few emotional bonds with each other? I think not. Men, I believe, can be quite deeply bonded to each other without the kind of sharing of thought and feeling that is so much a part of women's friendships and that we associate with the word "intimacy." To understand their relations with each other, however, we must distinguish between bonding and intimacy.[14]

It's not an easy distinction, nor is it generally understood. Perhaps it can be seen most clearly in the bonding between parent and infant, a connection that's as profound as any we know in human life. Yet we don't think of this relationship as an intimate one. For intimacy, as we think of it, is possible only between equals, between two people who have both the emotional development and the verbal skills to share their inner life with each other.

Between adults, bonding can signal the beginning of intimacy. But bonding also can live quite robustly without intimacy —an emotional connection that ties two people together in important and powerful ways. At the most general level, the shared experience of maleness—of knowing its differences from femaleness, of affirming those differences through an intuitive understanding of each other that needs no words—undoubtedly creates a bond between men. It's often a primitive bond, a sense of brotherhood that may be dimly understood, one that lives side by side with the more easily observable competitive strain that exists in their relations as well.

Then there's the bonding of two particular men to each other. The mates of the rugged Australian outback and the American wartime buddies, for example, have been extolled in song and story as men who have loved enough to lay down their lives for one another. According to Australian anthropologist Robert Brain, mateship is explained in much the same way as the relationship between our wartime buddies—a relationship between men who must depend upon each other for their very survival in a setting from which women are excluded.[15] In such situations, mates or buddies are, without doubt, likely to become deeply bonded to each other, providing protection, companionship, loyalty and devotion. When life itself is at stake, they may even drop their guard and share their innermost hopes and fears.

But how many of these wartime friendships are maintained as intimate relationships when lives return to normal? Margaret Mead, writing after our last heroic war, World War II, noted that English observers watching American buddy relationships were confused by the fact that our soldiers seemed to suffer intense grief at the death of a buddy yet, on close examination, the relationships were found to be extremely transitory. "[The] men," Mead wrote, "actually accepted their buddies as derivative from their outfit, and from accidents of association, rather than because of any special personality characteristics capable of ripening into friendship."[16]

Among the men I met, not one veteran of the wars in Vietnam and Korea retained anything more than a superficial relationship with the buddies who were so important to them then. They sang "Auld Lang Syne" together when they met, stirring fond memories and reawakening the emotional bond for a moment. But there was no intimacy between them.

A recent film, *Uncommon Valor,* showing how readily men who shared a war drift apart when they come home, graphically underscores the point. Watching the film, we come to understand that the emotional experience of the war remains deep. But the bonds between the men are brought to life only when they are called upon to join in another heroic task. In the years between, they maintain no contact whatsoever, losing track of each other, as if they had been no more than casual acquaintances.

And finally, a study reporting on the psychiatric treatment of Vietnam veterans over the last thirteen years shows quite plainly that the death of a buddy does not bring mourning for the loss but an infantile rage at the rupture of the fusion with this person who seemed to offer some magical protection. "The buddy's death . . . served as a premature loss of an essential and life-sustaining transitional object . . ." the author writes. "[An] indicator of the magical nature of the buddy-soldier relationship is that following the military, most veterans do not contact their buddy. It is as though that special, magical, and idealized relationship would be shattered were the soldier to really know the mundane realities of his buddy's life, what his buddy really loves and values, independent of the soldier."[17]

Only when we separate bonding from intimacy can we explain these relationships. Only then can we understand the friendships we sometimes see among American men, especially in the working class—relationships which seem at once so intensely connected yet so lacking in verbal expression. In this research, I came across a few such friendships, where all kinds of activities from work to play were shared, where the depth of the bonding was undeniable, but where feelings, whether about one another or about self, were given words only when tongues were loosened by too much drink.

An automobile mechanic, thirty-one years old, told this story of a friendship with a man who, he said, is "like my third brother." They met on the job where they worked together for two years, then left it to start a repair shop of their own, which was only marginally successful. After three years of struggling to make it in their own business, his friend, tired of what he called the "rat race in the city," was moving to a small town several hundred miles away. As the man I was interviewing told of the impending move, he turned his head away, not wanting me to see the moistness in his eyes.

"It must be very hard to think of losing Mike," I commented.

"Yeah, well, I know I won't lose him, just like I wouldn't lose one of my brothers if they moved away. We'll always be friends. But I sure will miss him."

"Have you and Mike talked about how it will feel to be separated?"

Quietly, "No, not really."

"What does 'not really' mean?" I asked.

Somewhat impatiently, "Just what I said, no."

"I know it's hard to talk about this kind of thing," I observed, "but could you try to tell me why not?"

"I don't know. I'm sure he knows what I feel. It's totally not necessary to tell him. I know in my own mind that he knows how I feel, and I know how he would feel if it was me going. So what's there to talk about?"

"So neither one of you has ever said to the other, 'I'm going to miss you'?" I probed once again.

"Well, I don't know; I wouldn't say it that way exactly. We both think about it a lot. So we talk a lot about how I'll come up and help him build his house or his shop up there, things like that. A couple of nights ago we had a little too much to drink, and he let it be known that he'd miss me, and I let him know too."

"What do you mean when you say you 'let him know'? What did you say?"

"Nothing much. He kind of said, 'Dammit, you're a buddy and I hate to go.' And I said, 'Yeah, yeah, I know what you mean.' So we both knew. I kind of wondered about it afterward, I mean, whether maybe he had an insecurity or thought I wouldn't miss him and he had to find out. But now he knows for sure."

I found myself fascinated by the sensitivity to emotional nuance with which he was able to think about this conversation with his friend—fascinated, and also struck by the internal constraints that kept these men from giving expression to their feelings. There weren't many conversations like this because few relationships among men match the intensity of the feelings this one generated. But by the time I finished talking with those few I encountered, I came to believe that the nights of drinking together that are so common among these men come not so much out of a desire to carouse but, at least in part, out of an inchoate wish to relax some of the constraints that bind them in their human relationships.

It would be a mistake to conclude that such relationships are given to working-class men alone, that feelings and fears are more overtly expressed among the educated middle class. It just isn't so, as this dialogue with a thirty-six-year-old university professor, who spoke insistently and passionately about men's relationships with each other, shows:

> I think the women's movement and all the talk about men not relating to each other is a crock. I don't think they understand about the kind of connection men get from the kind of sharing they do.

"Could you explain what you mean?" I asked.

A lot happens in the process of the kind of playing men do together. There's a tremendous amount of vulnerability and intimacy when you're out there playing tennis or basketball together. I cherish it greatly and so do a lot of other men.

"Again, I need to ask you to be more explicit. What do you mean when you say that there's intimacy and vulnerability when you're playing basketball?"

You're exposing a great deal about yourself in that kind of play. It's a way of expressing so much of who you are. If you get competitive or you get angry, you can't disguise it because you're acting spontaneously when you're playing a sport like that. The kind of person you are just gets expressed whether you like it or not.

[*Speaking heatedly*] Dammit, the ideal that women put out doesn't make it for men, that's all. There's a comfort that men have with men that's very different from what the women's ideal is, and I don't think they appreciate at all what the male ideal of friendship is about. There are other forms of intimacy than sharing feelings directly. The imagery that comes to my mind is Huckleberry Finn and Tom Sawyer, for example—that kind of deep sharing of doing things together. There's the intimacy of people who play together and work together that's very powerful and that creates very lasting bonds.

"You talk about lasting bonds in work and play. Yet it's my understanding that once the shared activity is gone, the connection is usually gone as well. Are you saying that's not true?"

[*Becoming quieter*] Well, maybe they don't continue to see each other once the activity doesn't keep them together, but that doesn't mean they don't share very deep and lasting bonds, does it?

Such words tell us, I believe, that there's comfort for men in the very nonverbal quality of their friendships that women decry—comfort in the belief that intimacy can be theirs without words. But many men also described their relations with others like themselves as a "two-edged thing."

Their friendships, they said regretfully, don't allow for much verbal intimacy or for certain kinds of emotional display. For that, they usually turn to the women in their lives. Yet these same relationships that disappoint them at one level are deeply gratifying at another. So they talked also of the relief they experience in relating to men because they don't have to "put out a line," because they're not "looking for conquest," because their similarities make for a sense of fraternity, because they permit shared understandings around being male and a kind of empathic responsiveness to each other they cannot experience with a woman.

There's romance in their words, and an almost mystical quality to the attachments they try so hard to describe—attachments that seem clearly to lean heavily on the kind of bonding I have been speaking of here. But bonding is not intimacy. Intimacy requires some greater shared expression of thought and feeling than these friendships exhibit, some willingness to allow another into our inner life, into the thoughts and feelings that live there.

I don't mean to suggest that intimacy always calls for words. Assuredly it does not. We have all experienced the warmth and intimacy of a companionable silence, of a shared task that's done without words yet where hands and heads work in a synchrony of mutual understanding. But, except perhaps in some rare instances, such understandings are possible because of the words expressed in the past, because of the sharing of internal selves yesterday that makes words unnecessary today.

There were, of course, some few men—only fifteen (10 percent) of those I interviewed, most of them men who were not married or living with a woman—who told of friendships with other men that included the kind of intimacy and sharing of self that, when it exists at all, usually is reserved for women. In a moving account of the process by which he came to develop such a friendship, a forty-eight-year-old writer talked about the impact of the feminist agitation in making him conscious of the meager emotional content in his friendships.

> I've known Elliot for years, since the sixties, but in the early times it's not very clear to me what kind of relationship we had. I don't think either one of us thought about such things then. The turning point was when he went to the hospital for an operation. I didn't know what kind of operation it was going to be or how serious it was. But I remember being very struck, when I went to visit him the day before the surgery, with the possibility that something could happen to him.
>
> I have to stop, however, and say that this all must be put against the background of women and the movement having raised the issue of how difficult it is for men to deal with feelings and to have any kind of expressive relationships with each other. It was a period when the movement caused a lot of men to reflect upon themselves. And I was in that process of looking at certain of the masculine characteristics in myself and deciding there were some I didn't really like.
>
> But the first time I really understood clearly what the women were talking about was on that evening when I went to visit Elliot. I remember having this conversation with him that felt very distant, almost strangulated. He never spoke about his fears; I never told him that I was concerned for him. It was such a male conversation.
>
> After I left, I realized that I had an enormous amount of feeling for him that wasn't expressed. I was taken by surprise. I never knew it until he was in this situation where he seemed at risk. He must have felt somewhat the same way because, after that, we both made an effort to get closer and to share more of what was going on inside ourselves.

Another man, a thirty-seven-year-old psychiatrist, read an early draft of this manuscript and wrote to me saying:

> The heart of the problem for men in forming friendships is reciprocity. Of the close male friendships I now enjoy, all but one

> started with the same pattern: I reached out to the person several times and became resentful because he never reciprocated. I mean, he never called to ask me to do something with him or to check on how I was doing with some problem I had discussed with him. My impulse was to give up, but Gail, my wife, was in the background, urging me on every step of the way. She'd say things like, "You can't stop now. Why don't you tell him you're hurt and see what happens?" So I did. Eventually I learned how to do it without her egging me on, and also taught the other man something about how to be a friend. I criticized or challenged him—often repeatedly—until he finally caught on to what I was asking of our friendship.

As I read these words, I thought about my own husband, who, for years, had been in much the same position. He had talked occasionally about envying my friendships, had made some attempts to establish relationships with men he knew. But somehow it didn't work. As my work on this project progressed and I got more and more caught up in the issues of men and their friends, it occurred to me that there were some things I could do to help him break through the barriers that kept him from having the friendships he wanted.

A few days after these thoughts came to mind, an incident occurred that gave me a chance to test out my resolve. I reported to him that I had talked to a friend who told me her husband, a man he likes very much, was ill. A day or two after that, he asked me, "Have you talked to Nancy? How's Jim?" In other times, I would surely have had an answer to the question, but this was what I was waiting for. "I don't know; I haven't phoned," I replied. Surprised, he looked at me and said, "Aren't you going to?" "No," I said. "Jim's your friend too; you call. If you really mean you want friends, this is a good place to start."

In the months that followed, we had many such conversations—I, consistently urging him to take the next step; he, always ready to take it once he could see the path. In the process, I came to see how, in my willingness to do what was so easy for me—that is, to take responsibility for maintaining our mutual friendships—I had unwittingly helped to keep him feeling helpless and inept in this arena. Now that I wasn't doing it anymore, he had no choice.

He now has some friends he can call his own—men he sees for lunch or dinner, men with whom he keeps in regular telephone contact when he can't see them, and with whom he shares some part of his inner life and thought, even his fears and anxieties. As with my colleague above, the men he chose to befriend didn't always know how to reciprocate. But he kept at it with a gentle persistence that has rewarded him with a few friends who no longer wait passively to hear from him, with whom there's a mutual sharing of lives and affection that has enriched all of them.

In one way or another, then, some few men have found their way toward more intimate relationships with other men. But most of these men spoke also of being "guarded," "skittery," "uncomfortable," "controlled," in the presence of any request for intimacy that seemed to be "too much." As one forty-one-year-old salesman put it:

> I have a couple of good friends I talk to about the deeper things inside me. But I don't exactly gallop into those areas. I go slow and easy and make sure I can stop when and how I want to.

Another man, a thirty-eight-year-old dentist, who talked about very good friends with whom both joy and pain have been shared through the years, warned:

> But one thing should be said here. That unguardedness and openness never happens when any three of us get together, even when Paul, who can be like a hysterical woman when we're alone, is there. Then we all act very much like any men do when they meet and talk. There's a kind of showing off, of being worldly-wise, being sexually a little raucous and telling stories of our ex-

> ploits. There's talk about "them," meaning women, and "us," meaning men—all that kind of manly talk that's so natural among men when they get together.

The fact that the interaction changes when a twosome becomes a threesome is no cause for surprise. The same is true of women as well. But that the content of the conversation so quickly moves to this kind of typically masculine display tells us much about the ways men protect themselves with each other.

"Who would you turn to if you came home one night and your wife [husband/lover] announced she [he] was leaving you?" I asked everyone who was married, living with someone or in a love relationship.

Almost always, the women had an answer that came readily to mind and tongue. Almost always, they named at least one friend, sometimes several, to whom they'd turn in that moment of shock and pain. Sometimes they mentioned some member of the family as well—a sister who was close, a mother or father who could be counted on—but never to the exclusion of friends, always in addition to them.

Not one woman was wholly without friends to whom she could turn for emotional support. Only two gave even the slightest indication that they would have difficulty in allowing themselves to mobilize these resources at once. Quite the contrary. "As soon as I picked myself up off the floor, I'd be on the telephone to Betsy," said one of the women in a remark that was typical.

But hearing the same question, most men sat in an uneasy silence for what seemed like a long while. When they finally found their voice, they spoke hesitantly as they realized there was no friend to whom they would turn at such a moment, none to whom they would reveal their anguish. A few thought of family—a sister, a mother, much more seldom a brother. One thirty-year-old California man who, earlier in our conversation, had talked about his several "very close friends" to whom he would go "for just about anything," said he would call his mother in Michigan.

"What about the good friends you were talking about a little while ago? Wouldn't you go to any of them?" I asked in surprise.

"Sure, sure I would," he answered quickly. "But first I'd have to put myself together—you know, get over the first shock so I wouldn't be falling apart."

Why? Why is it that a woman will "fall apart" with a friend and a man will not? What does it mean to a man to say, "I have a friend," if he dare not show himself in pain and vulnerability until he can "get over the first shock"?

5

Understanding Our Differences

By the time children are in their preadolescent years, the friendship patterns of girls and boys are already quite different. "While boys tend to view the group as a collective entity, emphasizing loyalty and solidarity," writes Zick Rubin in *Children's Friendships,* "girls are more likely to view the group as a network of intimate two-person friendships."[1] Boys, according to Elizabeth Douvan and Joseph Adelson, the authors of an influential work on adolescence, need "a band of rebels" to support their struggle against adult authority, while girls, who are more concerned with emotional intimacy, seek "a source of support and a repository of confidences."[2] Even as early as fifth grade, the research of sociologist Janet Lever shows, boys travel in bunches, girls in pairs.[3]

Until quite recently, such differences between girls and boys were accepted by most as ordained by God and foretold in nature. With the rise of an articulate feminist movement, a new scholarship developed that pointed quite convincingly to the ways in which these and other sex-stereotyped behaviors are shaped and maintained by the mandates of the culture—social conventions so long established and well entrenched that they have come to seem natural to most of us. Whatever the biological differences might be, feminist writers argue, masculinity and femininity are also social constructions which are defined differently in different cultures and at different historical moments. Thus the imagery those words carry and the behavioral expectations they call up are specific to time, place and culture.

The theory that boys and girls are socialized differently, therefore develop different ways of being in the world, is by now so well known that it needs little repeating here. We know that boys are raised to be tough, active, independent and emotionally controlled, while girls are taught to be tender, passive, dependent and emotionally available. We know that boys are not supposed to cry, even when they're physically hurt, while girls are permitted great leeway to express either physical or emotional pain. We know that boys are expected to be difficult and rebellious, while girls, it is believed, will be sweet and compliant. We know that girls are trained to nurture and boys to assume they will be nurtured.

From earliest childhood on, all these expectations are reinforced in a wide variety of ways—from the exhortations and scoldings of parents, the expectations of teachers, the images of men and women that come to them through the media, the games they each play.[4] Boys, trained in competitive team sports, learn young to value group cooperation and interpersonal competition. Friends "play" against each other. Lever tells us that, while the fifth-grade boys she studied might have strong friendships, "A boy and his best friend often find themselves on opposing teams."[5]

To win for his team a boy beats his best friend and *his* team. It's one of those difficult binds in life where winning means also losing something precious in the relationship with a friend. For it is not likely that the two will compete on the football field and have a close and loving relationship off it, not likely that they can put on a show of invincibility during the game and share their fears and vulnerabilities after it.

Not very different, is it, from the world of work for which he is destined—the world of large-scale organizations that now dominate modern industrial life and where team cooperation and the competitive spirit are equally valued? Not very good training, is it, for the kind of sharing of self and emotional support friendship requires?

Competition—a theme that runs through men's relationships with each other, one that kept coming up again and again as they sought to explain the lack of intimacy between them.

"You never know when another guy will come along and knock you off."

"Competition's the name of the game, so you kind of watch your step with a man."

"Whether you're bowling or going after a woman, there's always winners and losers."

"The last time I had any really close relationships with guys was in high school, when we were still boys, not men. After that, the competition thing gets to you. You compete for grades in college so you can get into grad school. Then you compete for a job and a promotion and a woman and . . . Christ, it never ends."

Even men who are now struggling with these issues, quite consciously, men who clearly recognize the cost to their interpersonal relationships of their lifetime of training for this kind of competition with others, spoke of the difficulties in trying to change.

"I don't like to admit it, but I get envious and competitive with other men. I'm working on it, but it's hard."

"I try not to get into that competitive number with my friends, but it's damn hard to change—damn hard."

The finely tuned competitive spirit that's so much a part of male life is alive and well no matter where men are or what they're doing. Over the years I have watched it at work in my therapy groups, where the differences in the men's and women's behavior with each other are striking.

When a new group starts, one of the first things the women do is exchange phone numbers, not something the men think of until the women push them into it. While the women make affiliative moves toward each other, the men make competitive ones. Both men and women may hope to be the favored patient, want to say the cleverest things, but the women try to contain the wishes, the men are in active contest to make them come true.

It isn't that the women don't have competitive feelings, only that they have much more difficulty in acknowledging them, therefore in acting on them. Yet their inhibitions about competition can damage their friendships almost as much as men's facility with it harms theirs. Indeed, it's precisely because women have, for so long, been constrained from expressing their competitive strivings cleanly and clearly that they can become distorted into the kind of petty rivalries, jealousies and envy that sometimes infect their relationships with each other.

With men, the competitive thrust is overt and direct; with women, it's hidden from view, too often covered over with a smile, with a veneer of warmth and friendliness that bodes ill for the kind of trust a friendship requires. A twenty-six-year-old single woman, a beautician, spoke both about the warmth of her relations with other women and about her wariness with them. After a long discourse about how important her women friends are in her daily life, she concluded, laughing:

> I guess you could say some of my best friends are women, but I don't always trust them. I mean, sometimes a woman can be your friend and also stab you in the back.

"Can you explain what you mean?" I asked.

> Sure! Suppose both of you have your eye on the same guy. Is she going to tell you she's out to get him? No, she'll just go after him and then behave like she's little Miss Innocence.
>
> Or even my mother—she's a terrific cook, so people are always asking her for recipes. But she never tells it to them right. She doesn't say no, she just leaves out something so it won't be as good as hers. I mean, why can't she just say she doesn't want to give it out because she wants to be known as the best damn cook around? What's wrong with that?

"What *is* wrong with that?" I asked. "Can you comfortably admit to your co-workers that you want to be a better hairdresser and, therefore, won't tell them about some great new product you just found?" Wrinkling her nose in a gesture that said she didn't like the question, she answered:

> Okay, I get your point. But dammit, I wish it didn't have to be like that. It spoils things. You have to go around hiding what you feel, then you do something you don't feel very proud of, or if you don't do it, you get mad and then end up doing something that's maybe worse.

It's such "minor spoilings," as one woman called them, that, when they could talk about this subject at all, women mentioned most often. The story of this thirty-three-year-old woman, who had been out of the labor force since her first child was born eight years earlier, was typical of those who made such comments:

> I told one of my very closest friends about a wonderful job opportunity that had just come my way, and there was this funny kind of silence for a minute. It made me anxious and uncomfortable, like I wanted to take the words back.
>
> [*Sighing*] I understand. She's had a job she doesn't like for years and can't seem to find another one, and practically the first time I walk out of my house, I get this great offer. But it spoiled my pleasure, and I was more careful about telling other people.

The moment of hesitation before she can express pleasure at the success of a friend, the slight withholding of an honest compliment, the too easy "You look wonderful," when it clearly isn't true—all create a breach, even if only a small one, all raise fears of envy, questions of trust.

But even when such behaviors are not at issue, women's inability to deal directly with competitive feelings is a source of difficulty in their relations with each other. For whether the motive is to compete or to avoid competition, it creates a similar distance between friends, as an event in my own life a while ago reminded me.

A friend and I were uncharacteristically out of touch for a long while. I thought about her from time to time, wondered why she didn't phone, noticed that I wasn't calling her either. But somehow it took over two months before I managed to break the silence between us with a phone call and a suggestion that we have dinner before a meeting we were both expected to attend.

As always, we felt warmed by each other's presence, enjoyed each other's company—enough so that, by the end of the meal, I was able to say, "Is there some reason why I haven't heard from you in so long?" She looked away for a moment, looked back at me and said haltingly, "Well, yes, but I'm a little ashamed to say it. I thought you might be feeling something about the fact that my book was reviewed in the *Times* and yours wasn't. It made me so uncomfortable that I just couldn't pick up the phone. But you didn't call either, so something *must* have been going on for you."

I sat silently for a long moment, taking in what she had said, processing what was going on inside me, trying to order both thought and feeling. And suddenly I knew what my part in this charade was. "Of course, I had some feelings about that, but they had nothing to do with you or with what kept me from being in touch. I did call when I read the review and told you how pleased I was, and we agreed we'd talk again soon. But it was around that time that I had started a new book, and the writing was going well and easily. I knew you were having trouble writing and feeling terrible about it. If we had talked, it surely would have come up, and I was afraid it would feel insensitive to you or one-upmanship or something."

We sat there staring at each other for a long moment, trying to register fully the impact of what each of us had said. Then we started to laugh, both of us realizing the lengths to which we had gone not just to protect the other but to cover up our own competitiveness. For once the words were spoken, it was clear that we had acted out of some mix of feelings, both generous and competitive. And it was also clear that we could own the generosity but had to deny our competitiveness and project it onto the other.

It's a paradox, isn't it? Because we're women, we have learned to abjure competition, have been taught to believe it to be a destructive force in human relationships, especially when it arises between us. So rather than acknowledge our competitive feelings—yes, even the wish to best one another sometimes—we distance ourselves from the object of competition, thereby damaging the very closeness we wish so much to protect.

Interestingly, women respond quite differently to their competitive strivings with a man than with a woman. I don't mean to suggest that most women rush eagerly into the competitive field with men. Far from it. But this, I believe, is largely because, after a lifetime of internalizing the social definitions of woman and her deficits, most women are convinced that their efforts would be doomed to failure. Most, but not all.

Many women are now in struggle against those definitions of self; many are now willing to enter into competition with men. I am speaking here not only about *behavior,* however, but about the *feelings* we allow ourselves to acknowledge, even when we know we won't act on them. And on this, both my research and my clinical work leave little doubt that a woman is less likely to deny her feelings of competitiveness and envy with a man, less worried about protecting him from them, than she is with a woman.

It's not, I hasten to add, that women are, in fact, so fragile as their fears about each other would make them seem. In the culture of women, however, the *expression* of such feelings as envy and competition is unacceptable. Partly this is a response to the messages we get from the world we live in—the world that lauded Walter Mondale's competitive spirit as he fought off contenders for the Democratic party's nomination for the presidency in the 1984 election, but complained that Geraldine Ferraro put herself forward for the vice-presidential nomination too aggressively, too competitively, that her pleasure in achieving her goal was unseemly.

But these real-world lessons find such fertile soil because they rest on earlier, more primitive ones—on a girl's earliest rivalrous feelings toward mother, on the fear and foreboding that once came with the wish to compete with her. As a small girl, this was the forbidden territory, the one that posed the greatest threat, not just to her but to mother as well. For along with the envy and the wish to compete was also the fantasy that she could win—a fantasy that brought triumph, it's true, but filled her with anxiety as well.

Such conflicting feelings arise out of the child's contradictory sense of self—the imagined omnipotence that competes with the certainty of utter vulnerability. At one moment, the child, in her grandiosity, can believe herself to be dangerously powerful, fully capable of besting or damaging mother. Partly this response is rooted in experience—an experience that makes possible the triumphant fantasy. After all, hasn't she had, by now, plenty of evidence that she could bend mother to her will, that her cry could make the breast appear, that her pleasure or displeasure would be reflected in mother's response?

But partly, also, the grandiose sense of self is the infant's response to her dependent helplessness, a defense against the knowledge that life itself depends upon another. Thus when, as can be expected with such defensive maneuvers, this one breaks down, the other side emerges. Now, instead of a grand and powerful self, comes the understanding of her own relative powerlessness in the world of adults who loom so large, who come and go so capriciously, seemingly so outside her control. And triumph turns to anxiety.

Add to this the fact that we all live with more than one reality, especially when it comes to the primary figure of our infancy

—mother. For all of us, there's the mother of the real world and the *representation* of her in our internal world. As the child grows, she comes to see her mother's relative powerlessness in the *real* world while, at the same time, she retains the image of the all-powerful mother in her *internal* world. For a girl to compete successfully with the real-world mother can bring one set of problems—the guilt at surpassing her, the fear that in doing so she may wound or crush the loved one. To win from the all-powerful mother of the internal world raises a different but equally difficult set of issues. For it signals the need to give up the belief that there will always be someone who can provide protection in an unsafe world.

Complicating all this is the depth and power of a girl child's identification with her mother—an identification that creates a sense of identity between them that makes beating mother dangerously akin to beating self. Often enough, for the adult woman as well as the child she once was, this feels like a victory that promises defeat.

In adulthood, a close connection with another woman is likely to reawaken the old fantasies and the feelings that accompanied it—the same envy, the same wish to compete, and the same combination of triumph and fear at the prospect of winning. Better to leave the field than to take the risk.

With a man, a woman can feel safer. At the most obvious level, because a woman knows that competition is common in men's relations with each other, she is freer to allow such feelings to emerge within herself. She knows also that while men may be fearful of women in the deepest layers of their psyche, in the real world of everyday life she's not considered much of a threat. Most men still think women are too emotional, too lacking in the capacities for reason and logic, to be worthy competitors in anything of consequence.

Less obvious is the fact that women and men are not, so to speak, playing in the same psychological ballpark. With a woman, as with mother, the likeness seems to carry some danger to both self and other; with a man, as with father, the difference seems to offer protection for both of them. There's relief in this—the relief of knowing that these feelings inside her are not damaging and dangerous, that he's strong enough to protect himself, just as her father always seemed to be. Envy and the desire to compete, therefore, need not be her shameful, fearful secrets, forever hidden inside while they leak out in the many covertly hostile ways women historically have had of expressing such feelings to each other.

As a psychotherapist, I believe one of my tasks is to help women to contact their competitive strivings more directly and to express them more openly, while at the same time helping men to mute them so that they can relate more freely and fully to each other. But I have learned also that this competitive spirit with which men meet each other will not be easily stilled —not with words of lament or disparagement, not with therapeutic intervention and understanding. Indeed, the speed and insistence with which it comes to the fore in men tells us that there's something important and satisfying in it for them.

I didn't hear much talk about this other side, partly perhaps because, in recent years, the negative aspects of their competitiveness has been so much the center of attention that it has become something of an embarrassment. But under all the discussion of the difficulties it causes in their relations with each other lies a clear sense of excitement and satisfaction for many men—the satisfaction of testing oneself, the thrill of pushing beyond limits already known, the excitement of winning. A thirty-six-year-old advertising executive gave voice to these feelings as he tried to explain the difference in his friendships with men and with women.

> For me, there's a certain ease in being around a guy. Number one, there's no sexual tension. Number two, I think we experience the world very differently from women. It's not that I don't feel comfortable with women, but I enjoy men in a special way. I enjoy

> competing with men. I don't like to compete with women; there's no fun in it. So I miss that part of it.

"What is it you enjoy about the competition?" I wanted to know.

> [*Laughing*] Only a woman would ask that. [*Then more seriously*] It's hard to put into words. I get to show off with men—I mean, I can strut my stuff, let myself go all the way. I really get off on that; it's exciting. It doesn't make much difference whether it's some sport or getting an account, I'm playing to win. I can show off just how good I am. Maybe they don't like to lose, but I get respect for winning. I'm good, really GOOD, and we both know it. It's a great feeling that you can only get when you've won against an honorable competitor.

Without question, understanding how we are socialized to our culturally mandated gender roles helps to explain such feelings about competition, helps to explain also why men have fewer intimate and self-revealing friendships than women. These processes by which we learn to play the roles our society has designed for us are powerful and effective forces in shaping human life—of that there is no doubt.

This, however, is not yet the whole story. It doesn't tell us why these socialization processes *take* so well, doesn't answer the questions that ask: What is the ground on which they are sown to produce such consistent results? Why is it that "boys will be boys" and "girls will be girls"?

For those answers, we must look to the traditional nuclear family itself and how children develop a sense of self and gender identity there. When we do, we see, as Nancy Chodorow has shown, that it is in the very structure of the family and the gender-related roles we usually play there that crucial differences between us are born[6]—differences, as I have explained fully in my previous work, that continue to create difficulties for us, whether in our friendships or in our love relationships with each other.[7]

I shall insist, however, that these differences between us are neither biologically nor psychologically given. At the most general level, my argument is that, from birth onward, psyche and society engage in a continuing dynamic interaction in which each of us constructs an internal psychological reality out of the material of the external social world.

For each of us, our internal world is created by our own sensibility, by the particular synthetic capability we bring to our experience. Thus it is that we can account for our individual uniqueness. Yet since we live in the same society, are raised with the same cultural norms, many of our experiences are shared. Thus it is that we can account for the common qualities among us. Only when we understand this dynamic interaction between society and the individual can we grasp how each woman or man is a unique individual with his or her particular way of experiencing the world, and at the same time, how we continue to behave so consistently in accord with the cultural mandates surrounding femininity and masculinity.

But what does all this have to do with friendship? How does it help us to understand the differences between women's friendships and men's?

Until now, I have argued that friends are central actors in the developmental drama, that they play a crucial role in the development of a full, coherent and satisfactory sense of self and identity. Now, in the pages that follow, I shall show also that the relationship between friendship and human development works the other way as well—that certain developmental requirements of early childhood are different for boys and girls, resulting in different structures of personality for men and women and, therefore, affecting the kinds of friendships they are likely to form in adulthood as well.

Classical Freudian theory tells us that the Oedipal rivalry with father is a boy's first experience of male competition—an experience that, in itself, undoubtedly marks his future relations with men. But there are developmental issues that arise well before the Oedipal period which go a long way toward explaining the lifetime intensity of that rivalry, not just with father but with all men thereafter.

As originally formulated, Freudian theory saw a single path in the psychological development of the child across which both boys and girls would travel. But as critics and followers developed and expanded Freud's original theory, new understandings emerged which showed us that the primary childhood task of developing an autonomous and bounded sense of self was even more complex than had been understood.

We now know that critical experiences affecting a child's ability to manage these developmental tasks successfully come in the earliest weeks and months of life, long before the Oedipal conflicts that so preoccupied Freud.[8] We know also that while the developmental imperatives are the same for children of either gender, the problems they encounter in executing the tasks before them are different for girls and for boys—differences rooted in the fact that mother, a woman, is almost always the primary caregiver of infancy. *No fact of our early life has greater consequences for how girls and boys develop into men and women.* Yet, until recently, we have taken it so much for granted as part of the natural order of the universe that we never gave it much thought.

To understand why and how this affects our development so profoundly, we must take a short journey into the psychology of infancy. As I have already said, most theorists of infant development now agree that, from the beginning, life is a process of forming attachments, internalizing people, things and experiences from the external world, shaping our mental representations of them, and making identifications with significant others in our lives. Since, from our earliest days on earth, it is mother who feeds us, shelters us, comforts us, holds us in her arms to allay our fears, it is she with whom we form our first attachment, she with whom we make our first identification, she with whom we become joined in a bond so deep that we are as one with her.

Parenthetically, the developmental literature usually refers to this relationship between mother and infant as a "symbiotic bond"—a term I, too, have used in the past without much thought. On reflection, however, I believe this is an inappropriate use of the idea of symbiosis—a concept that assumes a relationship of reciprocal need.[9] In fact, while a woman may form a deep psychological bond with her newborn, there is certainly no equality or mutuality of need between them, since a mother's survival is not dependent upon the relationship with the child.

It seems to me now that the widespread misuse of the notion of symbiosis in this instance is not just a semantic error but a product of the assumptions about the nature of woman and of the ideology of motherhood that have, for so long, held us in their grip. When motherhood is seen as woman's most natural function, the purpose of her life, the term "symbiosis" makes sense, since it suggests that a woman needs the infant as much as the child needs her—if not for her physical existence then for her psychological survival.

Certainly I do not wish to deny the importance of mothering in woman's life. In recent years, however, we have learned more about the complexity of women's internal needs and, in the process, have come to understand motherhood as one of several important functions for a woman, just as fatherhood is for a man. Most assuredly the biological ability to conceive, carry and feed a child makes for differences between a woman's psychological relationship to an infant and a man's. But equally certainly, our society's assumptions about the differences between *mothering* and *fathering*—about the different role each parent is expected to play—are central factors in the development of those psychological differences.

I am arguing, then, that the notion of symbiosis between mother and infant, and the unthinking acceptance it has gained, has served us poorly insofar as it perpetuates stereotypes about women and their needs while, at the same time, it leaves fathers standing helplessly and relatively uselessly outside the charmed circle. Indeed, this concept does nothing to illuminate either the differences *or the similarities* between men and women in their capacity for attachment and emotional connection with an infant, and nothing either to permit or encourage fathers to form the kinds of bonds that have been thought to be natural for mothers alone.

We would do well, therefore, to focus instead on the obvious fact of the infant's profound dependency, which directs us to a language that more aptly fits the inequality of need in the relationship, and not incidentally, embodies no assumption about biological or psychological imperatives in the mother. In doing so, we will also make more room for fathers' participation in this crucial stage in the development of the child.

As most families are presently constellated, however, our earliest and most primitive experiences of attachment and identification are with a woman. Whether a girl or a boy, it is a woman who becomes our first loved other, a woman with whom we identify as one like self, a woman whose representation lives inside us, the one the nascent sense of self will be measured against. This is the internal experience of infancy and early childhood that makes the future feel both safe and possible, the experience that seems to say to us, "This is who I am; this is who and what I, too, will be one day." And because it is a woman in this primary place in our internal lives, this same experience becomes part of the problem as we face the developmental steps ahead.

As early infancy passes, the need to separate from mother and to develop an autonomous sense of self comes to center stage in the unfolding developmental drama. This means, among other things, that the child must establish an independent, coherent and continuing sense of self—a bounded self that's unique and separate from any other. This psychological self is the internal analog of our physical self, not visible in the same way, but equally important to our sense of who we are. To negotiate the passage successfully two things must be accomplished: the crystallization and consolidation of an appropriate gender identity, and the development of what psychologists call "ego boundaries"—those internal psychological boundaries of the self that set us off from the rest of the world.

It's here that the problems they encounter are different for girls and for boys and, depending upon the issue in process at any given time, are sometimes harder for one, sometimes for the other. When the task is to establish the boundaries of self, the likeness between mother and daughter makes this more complicated for a girl than for her brother. Just because their gender is the same, it's more difficult for a girl to separate, harder for her or her mother to know where one begins and the other ends. On the other hand, when faced with the internalization of a gender identity, this resemblance between mother and daughter is a help, not a hindrance, while the difference between mother and son makes it a much more difficult and complicated issue for the child who is male.

For a boy who has been raised by a woman, the consolidation of his gender identity requires a profound upheaval in his inner psychic life. In order to identify with his maleness, he must relinquish his identification with his mother—the first person to be internalized into his inner psychic world, the one who has been so deeply embedded there as to seem a part of himself—and, in its place, seek an equivalent identification with father. This, I believe, is the origin of men's self-conscious concern with their penis as an organ of identity. When, as a small child, a boy must separate himself from his mother, it is the anatomical differences between them that can give some reality to the need, that make reasonable this demand that otherwise feels so *un*reasonable.

To protect against the pain wrought by this radical shift in his internal world, the child builds a set of defenses that will serve him, for good or for ill, for the rest of his life. This is the beginning of the development of the kind of ego boundaries so characteristic of men—boundaries that are fixed and firm, that rigidly separate self from other, that circumscribe not only his relationships with others but his connection to his inner emotional life as well.

For a girl, the formation of a gender identity requires no such wrenching breaks with the past. Since she need not displace the internalized representation of mother, there's no need to build defenses against feeling and attachment, therefore no need for the kind of rigid boundaries a man develops as a means of protecting and maintaining those defenses. This means that, as a woman, she'll develop ego boundaries that are more permeable than a man's—a fact of paramount importance in the management of both her internal life and her external one.

It's in this part of the developmental scenario that we see the birth of the empathic and relational capacities for which women are so well known, and which serve them so well in their friendships. Since she and her mother are the same gender, a girl never has to separate herself as completely and irrevocably as a boy must. As a result, her sense of herself is never as separate as his; she experiences herself always as more continuous with another; and the maintenance of close personal connections will continue to be one of life's essential themes for her. Consequently, she'll preserve the capacity, born in the early union with mother, for participating in another's inner life, for sensing another's emotional states almost as if they were her own—the capacity that, in an adult, we call empathy.

For her, too, there's little difficulty in giving verbal expression to her inner emotional life. Indeed, she'll reach for words as the surest way to sustain her connections with others—a difference between women and men that is one of the major sources of conflict and incomprehension between them.

A woman pleads, "Tell me what you're thinking and feeling." Her husband, bewildered, replies, "There's nothing to tell." A man shouts, "How the hell can you talk to Mary for so long?"

His wife, aggrieved, retorts, "I wouldn't have to if you'd talk to me."

For a man, these interactions are partly a response to the fear that the expression of emotion threatens to expose the dependency and vulnerability he has fought so hard to master. And partly they arise out of his distrust and wariness with a woman. For when, as a very small child, he had to renounce his earliest bond with mother, his inner experience was not that he had left the old familiar connection but that he had been left, that this mother on whom he had depended for life itself abandoned him to the shadowy and alien world of men—feelings that are not *just* a product of infantile fantasy.

There's fantasy, yes, but there's reality as well. The mother of a boy does, in fact, help him to make this separation with any number of reminders about the differences between them, about how he'll grow up to be a man like daddy, while sister Jane will be a woman like mommy. For the small child who, for so long, understood nothing of those differences—indeed, who saw himself as one with mother—her words feel like a betrayal, her actions like an abandonment. In pain and anger, therefore, he locks away the part of himself that had allowed him to be vulnerable to her, that had experienced dependency, that had trusted intimacy.

But there's yet another reason why words are not at the center of the definition of intimacy for men, why nonverbal activities will do at least as well, often better. Developmentally, the need for the repression of the identification with mother comes early in life, long before the linguistic ability develops sufficiently to permit the expression of complex emotional responses. For a man, therefore, there's an internal split between words and emotion—a developmental arrest that makes bringing the two together difficult.

It isn't simply that a man can't name his feelings; he's usually quite capable of saying he's angry, scared, guilty, and so on. Rather it's that he's left with a certain handicap in connecting words and feelings, experiences some difficulty in putting them together. Whether in a romantic relationship with a woman or in a friendship with a man, he can't easily describe and express the complexity of his internal emotional responses, can't readily talk comfortably about what they mean to him.

The need for close and intimate relations with others, however, is the very substance of human social life—a primitive need that will not be tamed by these acts of repression. Therefore, despite his efforts to stand apart, to keep himself tightly under emotional control, in adulthood, he's caught between his hunger to recapture the repressed part of himself and his guardedness in giving himself fully to any relationship whose intimacy and intensity are strong enough to call up the painful feelings of loss that accompany it. Because the heart and intensity of this struggle are connected to a woman, it's to her that he's most likely to turn as he seeks to resolve his ambivalence between need and fear.

This is why, for so many men, their closest friendships are with women. It's a woman, not a man, who taps the deepest levels of emotional need, a woman, not a man, who seems to promise relief from the pain of long ago, even while she also stirs the ancient anger and fear.

These differences about which I have been writing affect greatly the kinds of connections men and women can make with friends in adulthood. The boy child, whose developing sense of himself is so separate from others, easily learns to become the competitor. If relationships cannot be trusted to provide safety and security, then strength is the answer and winning is the goal. If emotions are dangerous because they make him feel that old vulnerability again, then reason and logic offer protection.

The girl child also is ready for the role learning that will be hers. With her permeable boundaries and clearly felt need for connection, she moves gracefully in the world of relationships, comes easily to the tasks of soothing and smoothing in order to make them work. For her, it's relationships that seem to offer safety, isolation that poses a threat. Consequently, if competition means distance, she'll reach for cooperation. If winning imperils relationships, she'll settle for a draw. If anger augurs danger, she'll remember to smile.

For both men and women, these are what psychoanalyst Heinz Kohut has called "compensatory structures"—internalized ways of being that usually can be only partially successful in coping with the deeper-lying unmet needs they are designed to serve.[10] For both, they undergird successes—his in what we have traditionally labeled the "affairs of men," the external world of work and authority; hers in what we call the province of women, the internal world of love and friendship. Yet neither finds in these defensive maneuvers the satisfactions they seem to promise. For the very psychological defenses that contribute to their successes also support their difficulties—his in the world of love and friendship, hers in the world of work and authority.

But this is not yet all. There's still another internal dynamic that, I believe, explains the depth and immediacy of women's emotional connections with each other—that tells us why their friendships remain so central in their lives—while helping us also to understand the distance men keep from each other.

The original infantile attachment and the identification that grows from it are much larger, deeper and more all-embracing than anything we, who have buried that primitive past in our unconscious, can easily comprehend. Their root is pure Eros—that vital, life-giving force with which all attachment begins. But we are a society of people who look upon Eros with anxiety and apprehension because it is associated with passion, with sex, with forces that we fear are out of our control.

Thus our young learn very early about the need to limit the erotic, about our fears that Eros imperils civilization. As infancy develops into early childhood, therefore, the social norms around sexuality begin to make themselves felt. In conformity with those norms, the erotic and the emotional components of attachment are split one from the other, and the erotic takes on a more specifically sexual meaning.

For a girl, the erotic component of the attachment to mother must be denied and shifted to a man if she's to grow up to be a heterosexual woman. But because a girl and her mother are both female, the larger emotional aspect of her attachment, and the identification that goes with it, remain undisturbed. In adulthood, then, the emotional aspect of any relationship will forever be the more compelling, the *basis* for the sexual connection rather than *result* of it, the underlying force in all her relationships, whether with a man or with a woman.

For a boy, this part of the developmental process, too, is quite different. Since identification and attachment are so closely linked, he cannot, as I have already indicated, repress his identification with mother without some attack on his attachment to her as well. Parenthetically, this is another source of the anger men carry toward women that often seems without cause. To make the assault, to sustain the separation, anger helps. But if he is to grow up to be a heterosexual man, the erotic component of his attachment is left intact while the larger emotional attachment lies wounded inside him.

The incest taboo, of course, assures that future sexual *behavior* will take place with a woman other than mother. I am not speaking here of behavior, however, but of the emotional structure that underlies it. And there, it's the erotic aspect of any attachment that will always hold the most immediate charge for him, the suppressed emotional part lying just below the surface of consciousness, ready to be brought to life by a sexual connection.

The origins of homophobia in men, the fear of homosexuality that's so common among them and that helps to keep men apart from one another, lie here. It's not that straight women open their arms to lesbianism any more than men welcome male homosexuality. But there's no doubt that women are not frightened by it in the same way men are. Partly that's because of the women's movement, which, after much struggle, has brought lesbians and heterosexual women together in a common cause.

And partly it's because women have a long history of close connections with other women—a history going back to the beginning of life when mother was the central figure of infancy.

For a woman, the emotional and the erotic are separated in such a way that she can be intensely connected emotionally without fear that this has anything to do with sexual desire. Thus, although a heterosexual woman may not be able to fathom the sexual attraction between lesbians, an emotional tie between any two women, gay or straight, is easily comprehensible to her. For a man, where such emotional connections generally depend on the sexual one, a close relationship with another man may well be experienced as a threat.

Add to this the fact that a woman's connection to her female identity is direct and continuous, firmly fixed in her earliest identification with mother. The sight of a "dyke," therefore, may cause a ripple in her consciousness, but it usually doesn't directly threaten a woman's sense of herself and her femaleness. Indeed, it was interesting to find straight women complaining that they felt neglected by friends who became lesbians and who now seemed to prefer relationships with others who share their gay identity. Speaking agitatedly, a twenty-six-year-old heterosexual woman said:

> Angie was one of my closest friends until she came out, but I don't see her much anymore. It's not my fault either; it's hers. She's so damned preoccupied with being a lesbian and her new lesbian friends, there's no time for me. It makes me mad. What's so special about being a lesbian that you have to abandon your old friends? [*Then more quietly*] It really hurts; she's been important to me for so many years.

On her side, Angie said:

> I care a lot for Julie; we've been friends since our first year in college. But I don't think she understands what it's like for me now. Coming out is hard as hell, and you need people who have gone through it around you; it comforts you. I can count on my lesbian friends to know what I'm feeling; with Julie I have to be

> explaining all the time. And then I'm not sure if she gets it or not.
>
> [*Pausing to think*] It's hard to explain; it's more than that. Being around women like me who I can like and admire makes me feel good about myself as a lesbian. Maybe I'm wrong, but when I'm with Julie I always feel like there's a question about me. I mean, the straight one is never in question, is she? [*Sarcastically*] She's "normal." She'd never say it, but it's what I feel. I talk about these kinds of things with my lesbian friends, and we try to be fair. We know that sometimes maybe it's our problem that we feel like that. But it's not *all* ours, that's for sure.

For a man, the connection to his male self is not defined directly by a positive primary identification with a male figure, but indirectly by the renunciation of the female—a circuitous route that makes for the kind of fragility in male identity that requires its constant protection. Consequently, the presence of a "faggot" can stimulate enough anxiety to move men to violent thoughts, if not acts. Indeed, for men, both lesbianism and homosexuality are experienced as a threat—homosexuality because it is a reminder of the insubstantiality of their own male identity; lesbianism because it impinges on what most men still *feel,* even if they don't always *believe,* is their birthright, a world filled with women whose main purpose is to serve and nurture them.

Gay men, therefore, repeatedly recounted the bitter experience of being abandoned by male friends once they came out. Sometimes the separation was gradual, as this story from a twenty-nine-year-old publicist tells:

> It didn't happen right away because he tried to be civilized about it. But he was uncomfortable with me from then on, kind of nervous. We made some efforts at continuing to be friends, and I think he tried to accept me, but he just couldn't do it. It was like I had a disease that was catching or something. I could feel him freeze up even just to shake my hand. After a while I guess we both decided we didn't need it. I certainly didn't; I was having enough trouble feeling okay about myself without him around.

Sometimes it happened quite abruptly, taking by surprise even someone who thought he had learned to be wary of the response of the straight world to the news of his homosexuality:

> We were finishing up law school when I got up the nerve to come out to a guy I'd known since high school. I didn't expect him to say "congratulations," but I didn't expect what I got either. While we were talking he tried to be cool, but he managed to be going the other way when he saw me coming after that. A couple of weeks later he had a graduation party and everyone we knew was invited but me.

The association of friendship with homosexuality is so common among men that, in the opening to his book on men's friendships, Stuart Miller writes that the first person he sought to interview, a philosophy professor, said to him, "Male friendship. You mean you're going to write about homosexuality? . . . Could be dangerous for you."[11] His second interview, this one with a science professor, began the same way: "You must be careful. You know, of course, that people will think you're writing about homosexuality."[12] "Everywhere I have gone," Miller says, "there has been the same misconception. The bizarre necessity to explain, at the beginning, that my subject is not homosexuality."[13]

In my own interviews, the anxieties of heterosexual men about homosexuality were much more hidden, rarely the subject of the kind of open discussion Miller reports—perhaps because he's a man, perhaps because so many of his interviews were held in San Francisco where the gay scene is so much a part of everyday consciousness. Whatever the case, I was never faced with the same "bizarre necessity" of which he complained. But this doesn't mean the issue wasn't present, only that, except in a few cases, I had to find it in inference and innuendo. For example, a forty-two-year-old high school teacher who had spent more than three years in a men's group, whose express purpose, he said, was "to learn to be closer and more open with other men," told this story:

We learned how to share some painful things at the meetings. Somebody could talk about it if his wife was giving him a hard time, and we could help him out. We even talked about sexual feelings. I don't mean that *macho* bullshit men talk about; I mean real feelings about sex and what it means and how it can make you anxious sometimes.

"How did this affect your friendships outside the group?" I wondered.

That's an interesting question. We started out as six guys who got together because we were having trouble with the women in our lives. They had been in a women's group for a long time, and we banded together, I guess, in some kind of defense—you know, to find out what this intimacy thing they were talking about all the time was all about. We learned some things, but it's funny, it never went beyond that room. I mean, we didn't get to be great friends. It's not like Lois, the woman I live with, and the women in her group. They're real buddies; they call each other up and talk for hours; they do things together all the time. We just never got that close, that's all.

"What did happen between you?"

When we were in that room, everything was up. We talked about work and love and kids. We even eventually were able to cry there. [*With a self-conscious laugh*] I have to admit, though, that nobody ever got very comfortable with it. It wasn't like when a woman cries and you could put your arms around her.

"Why couldn't you put your arms around a man who's crying?" I asked.

Aw, c'mon. I know you're kidding with that one.

"No, I'm quite serious," I assured him.

[*Squirming uncomfortably in his seat*] Men just don't do that, that's all; it's too uncomfortable. Christ, I don't know; I think there must always be some kind of a fear about getting physically close to a man. We used to hug each other when we got together, but even that [*pausing to find the right words*] . . . How can I say it? It was tight and self-conscious. You don't let your body go into the hug and the other guy doesn't either.

Another man, a thirty-five-year-old psychologist who was much more self-conscious about what he called the "homoerotic" element in some of his friendships, talked about the layers of feelings that are stirred up in these relationships:

I suppose there's a sexual tinge to every human relationship of any depth or intensity, but men are terrified of it. As for me, I've always been able to identify a kind of homoerotic quality to certain friendships with men. I don't mean that I feel a kind of frank sexual interest, but there's certainly something sexual about them. But along with that goes a very definite constraint. What I'm saying is that, with these particular men, there's both the sexual undertone as well as the constraint. And it's not just on my side; it works both ways.

"How do you know that?" I wanted to know.

[*With a broad grin*] It's easy. The greeting is the key to tell what's going on because there's both a letting go and a constraint in it. I mean, we greet with a hug or a kiss, and as soon as one or the other experiences the sexual tinge to it—or *thinks* or *fears* he's experiencing it—there's a slight backing off, an ever-so-slight gesturing that sets the boundaries and says, "This far and no further." I've experienced myself doing it, and I've experienced having it done to me.

This, then, is the gender story—a story of the differences between women and men that starts with the different developmental tasks we face when, as very small children, we begin the process of consolidating a sense of self and gender identity.

Most assuredly, I do not wish to deny the validity of the theories that point to the different role-learning and socialization processes for girls and boys. My argument is only that they do not go far enough in explaining why boys play in groups and girls in twos; why boys seem to fall so easily into competitive games and girls avoid them; why, for boys, the rules of the game transcend personal relationships and for girls they do not;[14] why, in adulthood, most men have "friends of the road," not "friends of the heart," while most women have both.

This lovely distinction was made by a colleague in one of our several discussions of the problems of researching and writing about a subject so ill-defined as to be almost evanescent.[15]

> Friends of the road are people who pass through your life. You don't know them forever, but only for relatively short periods of time. When they're there, they're there. But you have to buoy them up. If you lose contact, you lose the friendship because it's the contact that keeps it alive and vital. Without it, it goes stale.
>
> But friends of the heart are different. You don't have to buoy the friendship up to make sure it'll be there. It's like family; they're both just there. They're friendships that are long-lived and continuous. There's absolute trust between the friends; the relationship is fully reciprocal; and you don't have to be there all the time.

Friends of the road, then, depend on sharing time and place. When they're with us, they enrich our daily lives in any number of ways, providing many of the things we seek in our relations with each other—companionship, fun, intellectual stimulation, even, sometimes, emotional support. But we can count on them only so long as they are *in* our lives. With friends of the heart, the connection is more likely to take root around *being* rather than *doing,* around a sharing of self in ways that can be sustained apart from the accident of geography or historical moment. Since men are better at *doing* with each other rather than at just *being,* it makes sense that they would be less likely to have friends of the heart than friends of the road.

I insist, however, that we need not be fixed in these differences forever. But it will take some large social changes to make possible the psychological changes necessary to make a difference—changes, first and foremost, in the internal structure of the family and the roles we each play there. For until the traditional family is modified so that we have two parents who are the primary caretakers of our children, two who will nurture them from the moment of birth, so that they can have two figures with whom to make that early and crucial identification, the broad outlines of the patterns I have been discussing here will remain with us.

In such a family, a boy would be spared the difficult and painful experience of renouncing his earliest primary identification—an experience that forces him to erect boundaries which make intimate relationships, whether in love or friendship, difficult for him from then on. At the same time, his connection to his male self would be direct and continuous, defined positively by the primary identification with a male figure rather than negatively by the repudiation of the female—a difference that would free him to relate to other men with far less fear.

For a girl, too, the benefits would be large. With two figures of identification from the moment of birth, separation would be less fraught with difficulty and confusion in childhood, and the development of a well-bounded and autonomous sense of self less problematic in adulthood. Her relationships, whether with friend or lover, would be less muddied by conflict about merger, by the impulse to become one with another that she's likely to give in to in one moment and resist in another.

Certainly later events and other people make their mark as well, as anyone who has lived through these last two decades must see. Cultural prescriptions about masculinity and femininity shift, and we find ourselves struggling to claim parts of ourselves that were formerly hidden from view. To pave the way, we look for friends who will join us in the search for new ways of being, new ways of seeing ourselves and relating to the world.

But, as I have said, friendship and the developmental process are in a complex interaction in which sometimes one controls, sometimes the other. In these differences between men and women, it is the structure of the family, and the developmental imperatives that arise from it, that fix the boundaries of what's likely for each of us. We may expand those limits, of course, or contract them, depending upon the historical moment and the flexibility it allows in the definitions of feminine and masculine, in the roles we are each expected to play. And there's little doubt about the influence of friends in this process of stretching and testing. But until the structure of the family itself is changed, the outer limits at least will be fixed by the early developmental experiences I have described here.

Meanwhile, whether for women or for men, the path of friendship across the course of a life is an unsteady one, its importance waxing and waning depending upon the different life stages through which we pass. Of those, none has greater impact on our relations with friends than when we move from the single life to a coupled one.

6

From Singles to Couples and Back Again

A Rocky Road for Friends

Sex-segregated play is common in children from about three or four years old.[1] But it's not until later, in the years just before puberty, that the most striking separation occurs in friendship between the sexes—a separation that also heralds the beginnings of romantic longings for the opposite sex, at least for those who are destined for a heterosexual orientation. For those who will become homosexual, these first stirrings of romantic longing often are directed toward same-sex friends, leaving them confused, ashamed and struggling to deny internal needs in favor of external directives about the appropriate objects of sexual desire. But for the heterosexually oriented, friendship and romantic attachments live in a relatively peaceful and mutually beneficial coexistence during these immediate pre- and post-pubescent years.

Regardless of sexual orientation, these are the years when friends become a crucially important anchor in our lives.[2] Until then, as researchers Anne and Robert Selman have shown, the dependency and intimacy so characteristic of adolescent relationships are not a part of children's friendships.[3] For the small child, it's still a family member who hears the secrets, who shares the joys, who dries the tears, who provides a sense of continuity and stability. Even when younger children have close friends with whom they spend a good deal of time and energy, the family is still at the center of their lives.

Thus, important though friends may be in our early life, we are not yet emotionally dependent upon them, not yet deeply involved in their lives, nor they in ours. It isn't until the years just before adolescence that such attachments begin to characterize our friendships—that they begin to take on the urgency of necessity, that they can inflict almost unbearable pain and equally intense pleasure.

Relations inside the family at this time are likely to be fraught with the conflict of the struggle for independence. Separation, autonomy, identity—all are continuing themes, all reaching new levels of intensity through the adolescent years. To support the struggle, to ease the pain, to help in the passage, to share our secret hopes, angers, fears, fantasies and loves—for this we turn to friends.

This is perhaps the only time in our lives when friends come fully to center stage, transcending all other relationships in immediate importance as they engage with us on a daily basis around every aspect of living. Paradoxically, until this time, friends have been urged upon us at every turn. But from adolescence on, these very friendships will often be seen as outlaw relationships—as a threat first to the authority of the family, then to the stability of the marriage.

It's not just unreasoning parental anxiety that makes the peer relationships of adolescence seem problematic. These friendships do, in fact, practically take over the lives of the young, becoming highly influential in helping the adolescent to separate from the family, in providing a model for living that is different from, and perhaps antagonistic to, the values espoused there, in encouraging experimentation with ways of being the family may wish to constrain.

At the same time, these friendships have their own requirements for conformity that can be more rigorous than all but the most demanding and authoritarian family relations. Thus it often seems to parents that, despite their declaration of independence, the children have exchanged one kind of conformity for another—a situation that adds fuel to parental fears and to their doomed attempts to subvert the peer bonds their children establish.

The reality of these adolescent friendships is that they constrain and encourage individuality at the same time. The demands for conformity to peer group norms—whether in manner of dress, speech or behavior—act as a constraint on the expression of a separate or distinctive identity, while the support for parts of self the family is unable or unwilling to nourish provides powerful encouragement. This tension between individuality and conformity that lies at the core of these friendships is, in fact, a fundamental part of their reason for being, an external manifestation of the internal struggle of the developing child at this stage of life. For at the same time that adolescents struggle to separate from the family, they also find themselves fearful of the very freedom they keep insisting upon.

To calm their fears, to reassure themselves that they are not alone—for this, they turn to friends, giving over to them some of the freedoms they have wrested from parents. But all of it, the constraint and the freedom, is part of the testing of self the adolescent needs to undertake—part of the way the child learns to determine the boundaries of self, to find the space between conformity and rebellion that feels most comfortable, that permits the growth of individuality within the context of relatedness.

With the advance of puberty and the heightening of sexual interest and desire, romantic relationships begin to compete with same-sex friendships—a competition that friends eventually will lose. At this stage, however, these two sets of relationships remain entwined, with romance only temporarily winning out over friendship.

Both men and women recall vividly how the friends of adolescence served increasingly important functions in their developing interest in the opposite sex. They shared the fantasies, rehearsed each other for the real thing. Both tell of seemingly endless, consuming conversations about "them," of advice exchanged about how to attract the attention of a desired one, how to keep it once they got what they were after. Those who were lucky enough to have an older opposite-sex sibling learned something of the etiquette of dating and mating by watching and listening in the family. For the rest, it was friends alone who taught these essentials.

Women told of the friends who taught them what to wear, how to style their hair, how to apply the make-up that would heighten their attractiveness. They recalled the fun and excitement when a friend helped them dress for a date, all the while practicing with them how they would walk, what they would say, even how to kiss or refuse to do so.

Men recalled that they confided to friends their longings for the girl of their dreams. They rehearsed with them how to approach her, when to speak, when to keep silent, what to do if she said yes, how to act if the word was no. Even the bragging and posturing that's so common among adolescent boys was part of their induction, serving up clues and cues to the twin mysteries of girls and sex, and helping them to order their feelings and master their fears.

Among the heterosexually oriented, where the stirrings of sexual desire are connected to the opposite sex, a friend's preoccupation with an adolescent romance is understandable, even when it is also hurtful, mirroring as it does the longings inside self. But this is a particularly poignant and painful moment for those whose romantic longings are attached to the same-sex friend since, for them, the intensity of an opposite-sex attraction is difficult to comprehend.

Where the yearnings for the same-sex love were not yet experienced—perhaps because they were kept from consciousness by the dominant heterosexual norms, perhaps because they had not yet developed fully—these adolescents generally were able, as one man said, "to play the heterosexual game" without much more difficulty than their straight friends experienced. But for many men and women, the pull toward love relations with those of the same gender is part of conscious experience very early in life. For them, the difficulties of these years loom large and painfully in memory, as they tell of their struggle to deny the feelings inside them and to play out the heterosexual role that, even then, they knew was an alien one.

Whether straight or gay, however, friends will suffer the pain of loss as the exclusivity of their relationship is disrupted by another. But even at this age, the difference between the friendships of boys and of girls is already clear, a forecast of the shape of their future relations as men and women.

A girl and a boy may both have a best friend in this period, but the way these friendships are experienced—the intensity of the emotional connection, the importance they assume in the life of each—differs considerably. Among girls, such friendships take on a Siamese twin–like quality, so inseparable do the friends seem, so central to their well-being. Among boys, however, even best friendships are more emotionally contained, less insistently focused on the twosome, less deeply involved in each other's inner life.

For a girl, therefore, it is a particularly difficult and conflictful experience when the emotional intensity she has shared with a friend is diminished because a new love enters the picture. I say "a new love" because, irrespective of the sexual orientation of the girls involved, these friendships share many of the characteristics of a love affair, so obsessively are the friends entwined.

By late adolescence or early adulthood, romance wins out as the intense loyalties and deep attachments that bound us to same-sex friends wane under the force of the urge to mate that now rises so compellingly inside us. It's another of those ironic contradictions that friendship, which gains its power and force out of our need to separate from the family into which we were born, now becomes the casualty of our search for a new family —at least during the years when mate seeking and family building become the central developmental tasks of our lives.

Repeatedly, people recalled feeling betrayed and abandoned during these years, speaking of being "set on the shelf," "put on hold," "expected to sit around and wait," or just plain "dumped" when a romantic interest entered the life of a friend. So difficult are these experiences that, years later, people spoke of their anger and anguish with a vividness that suggested it all could have happened yesterday. Speaking with an immediacy that testified to the depth of his feelings then, a forty-year-old man told it this way:

> When my buddy Steve met this girl—Molly, I think her name was —that was it. No more hanging out, no more card games, no more goddamn friend. All of a sudden I had to call him up to make a date. No point going by his house like I did before, because he wasn't there. He was at her house. Christ, I can still remember how terrible I felt, like somebody died. I mean, they'd have a fight and he'd come around again, and they'd get together and away he'd go. But it was never the same. Who could trust him again after that?

Throughout the early adult years, the consistency and intensity of relations with friends depend on whether there's a love interest around. When there is, friends are expected to understand and accept that love is a more compelling priority than friendship. And while they often do—partly because they have no real choice, partly because they understand that the day will come when they will do the same—the lesson that's learned about where friends fit into our lives is not easily forgotten. Whether we are forsaken or forsake another, the message is driven home: Friends take second place.

If the late teens and early twenties are mate-finding time, the years that follow the wedding ceremony are family-building time. Friendship, while not unimportant, remains at the periphery of attention rather than at its center. Some friends are made, of course, but it's the more immediate relationships and problems of living that are the focus of attention. Making a living, raising young children—these are the tasks that preoccupy most people throughout these early years. One couple, thirty-one and thirty-two respectively, married ten years, she an assistant bank manager, he a loan officer in another bank, recalled the issues of that time. The wife:

> Just getting married and learning to live together was all we could attend to. We were both working, both very busy. We didn't really have enough time for ourselves and whatever responsibilities we had, let alone for friends.
>
> It's not even time so much, I guess, but the energy it all takes. It was important to get each other to the point where we felt satisfied that we really were more important than anyone else. That was an issue for both of us, I think.

Her husband told it this way:

> I guess you could say the first part of marriage is wonderful and terrible at the same time. I mean, I wanted to get married, but then when it happened, it was like, "Boom, gulp, here I am and I did it." So there are things you have to work out between you, and your friends take a back seat. With us, there was this thing where she wasn't crazy about my old friends and I didn't like hers so much either. She said just the other day, when we were talking about her interview with you, that now she doesn't think it was that we didn't like the old friends so much, but it was because we were jealous of them.

Here again, class makes a difference in how this passage is negotiated—how old friendships are dealt with, what new ones are made. Among working-class couples, who tend to marry young and who continue to live in the old neighborhood, this can be a particularly hard time. For these young people, the peer group attachments of the high school years are alive and well, the pull they exert, especially on the men, threatening to the marriage. The young wife, therefore, does her best to sever her husband's attachment to the group with whom he so recently spent so much of his time. A twenty-five-year-old woman, married seven years, remembered:

> The biggest fights we had when we were first married were over his friends. Those guys used to hang on the street all the time, or they'd run around doing things they're not supposed to do and get in trouble. They didn't care that Jimmy got married; as far as they thought, nothing was going to change. Well, they had another thought coming, and so did he. I wasn't going to be second to that gang of guys; that was one thing I wasn't going to stand for. I was going to come first or I wouldn't be around, and Jimmy knew that. So we fought, but I won.

When Jimmy tells his side of the story of those early struggles, it becomes clear that her victory was not without its costs to her friendships as well.

> The whole friends thing was a big deal when we first got married. Mary Claire didn't like the guys I used to hang out with, and we fought a lot about that. She didn't want them to come here, and she didn't want me to go out with them either. So then all that was left was her girl friends, and I didn't want them hanging around, yakking it up all the time. They'd come over and she'd get all excited. I used to think she was happier to see them than me. I mean, you know, I'd come home and she'd say "Hi" or something like that, but when one of them would come over, there'd be all this carrying on and laughing and talking and [*Searching for the right words*] . . . Hell, you know how women are.

The implicit bargain that's usually struck among such young working-class couples is that they both give up their old friends, although if she isn't working, she may continue to see hers during the day. This is at least part of how it happens that working-class couples spend their leisure time with kin so much more often than people in the middle class. It begins here in the first months of marriage when, having severed the old peer ties, they turn to parents and siblings for company.

Obviously friends don't have a monopoly on the wish to compete for the time and favor of the young wife or husband. Family members do their share as well, making claims that pull on old loyalties and obligations in ways that often create plenty of conflict in a new marriage. Still, whatever their troublemaking potential, both partners usually believe that parents and siblings have a stake in the consolidation and maintenance of the new marriage in ways that friends do not. Therefore, kin are experienced as less threatening than friends.

I don't mean to oversimplify these kin relationships and their functions in working-class families. As I have written in an earlier book on working-class family life, they remain in close contact for a variety of important reasons, not least of them the mutual helping relationships that have historically bound the members of extended working-class families together.[4]

When money is tight, socializing with family is cheaper and easier all around. There are no airs to put on, no embarrassing explanations to make. When there are children and both parents are in the work force, a grandmother may take over child care and get paid for it—an arrangement that benefits all concerned. Grandmother earns some needed income; parents are reassured about the care and training their children are getting.[5]

While working-class men and women tend to move directly from peer group to marriage, the young people of the middle class marry substantially later. Indeed, college-educated middle-class men and women live an entirely different script at this particular turning point in their lives. Once high school is done for them, few continue to live "on the old block," either physically or psychologically. Even if they live in the family home during college, the center of social life usually shifts from the neighborhood to the college classmates. By the time the four years of college are over, a new set of friends has been established, the old ones often falling away in what seems a natural result of different experiences and, more than likely, the discovery of new parts of self, of new interests and values.

These newly acquired friends are not necessarily lasting ones either. But they serve quite effectively at this life's juncture to separate young women and men from the old neighborhood-based relationships and to socialize them into the life they are about to undertake. Speaking of the disruptions in friendships that come with the march toward higher education and a career, a forty-eight-year-old physician said:

> People have entered and left my life a lot—no old neighborhood people in my life, nobody from high school, nobody from college, hardly anybody from medical school or my internship and residency.

"Can you say why that is?" I asked.

> Sure, everything was changing and moving because the emphasis wasn't on people. It was on social mobility and education and so forth. I didn't go to a neighborhood high school because the one on the other side of the city was where the smart kids went. I didn't go to a neighborhood college, and I guess there's no such thing as a neighborhood medical school. So from high school on, I was separated from the neighborhood kids. And everywhere along the line, I would meet a new group of people who I would then leave as I moved along. It wasn't until I finally settled down in one place eighteen years ago that I developed relationships that have been maintained.

Whenever they marry, however, and whatever their class, the early stages of building a new family usually find the young couple jealously guarding their turf—preoccupied with consolidating the new union, with reassuring each other and themselves that this new family comes first. The belief, so common in our society, that the new mate will satisfy all our needs makes it easier to set friends off to the side, to diminish their importance in the immediate afterglow of marriage when such expectations are highest. In a comment that was typical, a woman married ten years said:

> When I got married, I wanted to be Mrs. Perfect Wife–Mother–Married Person, and I pretty well locked out my friends. When I think about that now, I wonder [*her words trailing off*] . . . It's not fair to friends, is it? But when you first get married, you don't think about anything else really. It's like that becomes your life —for a while anyhow.

"What do you mean when you say you 'locked out' your friends?" I asked. "Did you stop seeing them?"

> I didn't exactly stop seeing them altogether. But my energies weren't with them the way they had been. They were tied up in my husband and getting a new life organized and [*pausing as she reached for words*] . . . You know how it is at the beginning. That's your *life!* How can a friend compete with that?

Most young couples maintain a social life, of course—an evening at the movies, the bowling alley, the theater, a concert, dinner together at home or out, picnics and partying, especially before the first child comes along. But even when some of those same activities formerly were shared with single friends, they are now largely coupled events.

At the start, couple friendships usually are held together by the connection between either the women or the men, the other mates going along because the relationship, while not close, has both its fun and its functional side. With time, such relationships begin to develop a history and rationale of their own, along with bonds that sometimes last through a lifetime, even if without the kind of intimacy and intensity all or some of the individuals in them may also crave.[6]

Often the couple friendship serves the two people who formed the original connection well. The joint social life the couples share gives meaning to the friendship for all four people and helps to make the individual friendship less threatening to those who stand outside it. As the couple relationship matures, the separate friendship also is strengthened by the bonds the foursome develops. When the original friends share both a social and a family life over an extended time, the relationship gains enough social and emotional anchors to expand the base of intimacy between the friends, thus helping further to assure the continuity of the friendship.

But couple friendships are not without their own problems and frustrations. Over and over, people spoke about the difficulties in finding comfortable and compatible relationships with other couples, about how hard it is to find four people who like each other equally well. It's hard enough to find two people who click on all the levels a close friendship requires, but a foursome who can make the necessary connections in all directions, they insisted, is rare indeed. A twenty-seven-year-old cook, married four years, complained:

> Sherry and I haven't been a couple very long, and I guess close couple friends take a long time to develop. I have one couple friend from when I was a single where I like both people a lot. But that doesn't mean that the foursome works very well. It gets a little lonely not having other couples you really enjoy.

The companionship that couples seek from each other is, however, only the most obvious of the ways these relationships serve a marriage. At another, less easily observable level, couple friendships are an important part of the social cement in a marriage, providing support not just for each other's marriages but for the institution itself. Our relations with others like ourselves validate the choices we make in our own lives. When we surround ourselves with others who are coupled, we begin to see the world as if that were the whole of it—a vision that reassures us even if, someplace inside, we know it isn't so.

Old single friends may be angered when a newly married man suddenly can't be counted on to go to a ball game or stop off for a drink after work, when a woman isn't as available as she used to be for a long telephone conversation, a shopping excursion or a movie. Married friends, understanding the constraints in their own lives, are more sympathetic with another's as well. Therefore, they're not as likely to intrude or to make difficult or unacceptable demands.

Friends who are married also tend to honor and respect another's marriage—indeed, to care about its survival—in ways that friends who are single usually do not. A problem between marital partners threatens the fabric of life of couple friends with whom they share close ties. Therefore, when it comes to the friends' attention, they are likely to view the problem with at least as much solicitude for the continuity of the marriage as for the individuals in it. Similarly, the very difficulty of having to confront friends with the news of an impending divorce keeps many couples together through a crisis that might otherwise shatter the marriage at once.

For those whose single friends are disappointed in them, or for those who may themselves be feeling twinges of restlessness with the confines of marriage, the empathic response and the shared estate of married friends gives consolation. We look around the neighborhood, and we're soothed by the knowledge that we're part of the mainstream of life. We have a good time with another couple, and our lives seem brighter and fuller. We notice that their conflicts are not too different from our own, and we feel safer. A forty-two-year-old woman, the director of a social welfare agency, married twenty years, commented with acid irony about these meanings of typical coupled social relationships:

> I used to wonder sometimes why we were doing this when we first got married. I'd think, "These people don't really know me and I don't know them. So what am I doing here?" But then I figured out that if you could get six or eight people, all married, sitting around in the living room and finding out that they were all living essentially the same life, and that they could all be accepted by

> each other, then they didn't have to wonder if they were crazy or something. If everybody's doing it, then it's okay for you to do it, too. It teaches you that this is what life is, so you won't complain and don't get antsy.

"It teaches you that this is what life is . . ." A neat summary of the way the social relationships with which we surround a marriage help to ease the strains of the transition to this new life, help to induct us into the stream of married life—and to keep us there.

It's not just among the newly married that couple relationships feel safer and more comfortable than independent friendships, as a look at what happens when friends get divorced shows so clearly. Sometimes, when divorced friends are unhappy, a continuing relationship with them serves to affirm us in our own marriages, to reassure us that our coupled state, no matter what its problems, is better than the single one. A twenty-eight-year-old woman, a bank teller who has been married for nine years, spoke quite openly about just this function of divorced friends:

> We have a lot of divorced friends hanging around all the time. Sometimes it's a pain, but they need a place and somebody to understand them, so mostly they're welcome here. When things aren't going so smoothly for us, it reminds us to appreciate what we've got when we see how bad things can be in their lives.

But when the lives of divorced friends don't seem filled with tragedy and loneliness, it's another matter. Then, time spent with them can heighten whatever ambivalence we have about the shape of our own lives. A thirty-eight-year-old man, married fourteen years, talked about the conflict he sometimes feels when he socializes with some of his colleagues who are divorced.

> A couple of the men I associate with at work are in the process of getting a divorce. We go out to lunch or have a drink after work

and I come away envying them their freedom sometimes and wondering why I keep my nose to the grindstone.

To relieve the discomfort and anxiety such feelings evoke, he hurries home looking for reassurance that his life, too, has its rewards:

> When I get home and I see the lights on in the houses on the street and know the people in them are doing what I'm doing, I remember that it feels good to be part of this world. I get in my house, and maybe Mari has fixed a nice dinner, and the kids are cute and wonderful, and maybe some friends come by for coffee, or we're going to a movie together, and I think, "Oh yeah, this is why I'm married."

Some people said that the bitterness their divorced friends displayed in the immediate aftermath of the rift made continued contact difficult. By the time the divorcing couple sheathed their swords and bound their wounds, the old friendship was so seriously damaged that it couldn't easily be put back together. Others were quite open about the fact that a friend's divorce raised anxieties about the future of their own marriage, that on hearing the news, their first thought was, "It could be me."

Given the feelings divorce can stir, it's not surprising that married couples tend to limit contact with divorcing friends, not surprising that, even after the first flush of anxiety is gone, married friends so often find it hard to make room in their lives for those who are divorced.[7] But being divorced is different for men and for women because a woman alone is even more likely than a man to be excluded from the social life of married friends.

A recently divorced or widowed man is apt to be an object of concern in ways that a woman is not. No one worries about whether a divorced woman is managing her household or her children, whether she's eating well or not. But let a man be asked to do the same things and people assume he needs help and offer it. A thirty-one-year-old mother of two small children who also works full-time as a legal secretary said with some bitterness:

> When we separated, our friends kept inviting Ken over to dinner on the nights he had the kids because they felt sorry for him. But I don't think it ever occurred to anyone to worry about me that way.

Moreover, unlike a woman, a single man of any age is a socially prized "commodity"—sought after as a companion, a dinner guest, a sexually desirable person.[8] My own husband, who, at forty, suffered the death of his wife, still speaks with surprise of the many attentions that came his way within hours after the funeral and continued for the four years of his widowerhood.

Even today, when so many of our traditional social attitudes are in flux, an extra woman at a party is still considered a burden in most social circles—as many women find out all too quickly when the phone stops ringing and they hear in the grapevine that their ex-husband was invited to a social event to which they had hoped to go. Indeed, some divorced men talked about having to "dodge invitations" to events that no longer interested them once they were single again—a complaint I rarely heard from a woman. A thirty-nine-year-old building contractor, divorced three years, said:

> When my ex-wife and I first split up, I think it was hard on everybody, including our friends. But then some people began to invite me over, mostly when they were having some kind of a thing like a dinner or a party, or something. It was okay at first, but [*somewhat embarrassed*] . . . Look, I don't want you to think I wasn't grateful, but after a while, when I got adjusted to being single, there were other things I wanted to be doing, that's all.

Finally, women are much more accepting of "man talk" than men are of "woman talk." Therefore, it's not nearly so discomfiting to most married couples to have a man visit for an evening as it is when a woman is there. When a man is the guest, the woman of the household usually has no trouble either joining in the conversation or sitting by quietly. But when it's a woman, the husband is likely either to dominate the evening or to feel left out, restless, bored—and show it.

Either way, it doesn't work well. If the husband's presence is felt too strongly, the guest feels cheated of a visit with her friend. If he withdraws into a restless inattentiveness, both wife and friend are equally uncomfortable. Faced with either of these possibilities, a woman may hesitate to invite her friend. Even if she does, the single woman is likely to refuse the invitation in an attempt to protect both herself and her friend from discomfort and embarrassment.[9]

It doesn't happen that way all the time, of course. There are today many men who are happy to be in the company of women, who find their conversation as stimulating as any they have with a man. But such men are still in a small minority, as the testimony of most women of any age and class shows quite clearly. Only eleven women of all those I met spoke of being fully comfortable when visiting a couple friend, and always it was with one particular couple where, they said, the man was "unusual," "a different kind of animal," "an especially sensitive person."

Sexual jealousies often become an issue as well. Husbands and wives are aware that the familiarity of marriage can be a disadvantage when in competition with the mystery of the unknown. Both, therefore, may look on somewhat uncomfortably as a mate interacts with a single person of the opposite sex. A husband watches suspiciously as an unattached friend seems to him to be too attentive to his wife. A wife fears that a single friend will look at least momentarily more interesting and exciting than she to her husband. When such feelings arise, the safest course for the marriage is to let the friendship go. "It costs too much at home to have lunch with a woman friend," said a thirty-six-year-old recently married professional man. Asked to explain, he shrugged:

> There's nothing to explain. Sandy gets jealous; then we have problems, and it's not worth it. Sometimes I get guilty when an old friend calls and I have to think up excuses; then I get mad at Sandy. But that doesn't help things between us either, so I just try to avoid the whole situation as much as I can.

But there's another side to this story about friendships between married folk and their single friends, a side much less often told. Without doubt, many single, divorced and widowed women and men feel abandoned and rejected by their married friends—a situation that can be particularly galling when there's a history of a warm and close relationship. Without doubt, there's justice in these complaints. What's less often told, however, is the part single people play in weakening the tie and widening the breach.

Some singles spoke about their discomfort in being with certain couples who seemed to stand inside a circle from which the two looked out as one. One thirty-four-year-old man described his experience this way:

> It's hard to explain, but some couples put out such a complete couple message that it's hard to be with them. You don't have any sense of being with two different people. It's as if they're thinking and acting in concert, as if they had one mind between them. It's very disconcerting to feel so excluded. It emphasizes my aloneness, and I end up feeling lonelier than when I'm actually alone.

Both men and women also complained about friends who, once they marry, seem to "become someone else," who are "no longer any fun," saying that they preferred the company of single friends who live under fewer constraints. Women spoke angrily about friends who "defer to a man," who "fade into the background."

> My friend Maureen is a good example. If we see each other alone, it's fine. But when she's with her husband, it's something else. It's like she's a stranger. She defers to him and hardly participates in what's going on. I feel like I'm having an evening with him and she's an appendage. All the single people I know have trouble with couples because they're so [*frowning as she struggled for the words*] . . . so damned coupled.

With equal heat, men denounced friends who are "henpecked" or "under her thumb," who "can't even stop for a beer without asking her permission."

> I used to have a best buddy; then he got married. I don't see him much anymore because it's a drag. He can't do anything without checking with that wife of his. Christ, it makes me mad.

While all these may be legitimate complaints, single people also often acknowledged that they are uncomfortable with married friends who give none of these offenses. For them, they said, it is simply the fact of being single in what feels like a coupled world that motivates their withdrawal from the friendship. Thus, even when invitations are offered, they refuse to join married friends in their activities.

I had such an exchange recently when, talking to a single friend who sounded lonely, I invited her to join us and another couple for dinner. She accepted my invitation warmly, letting me know she appreciated my concern. A few minutes after we concluded our conversation and I had turned my attention elsewhere, the phone rang again. "If you don't mind, I don't think I'll come after all," she said. "Why not? Did something more interesting come up so fast?" I asked. No," she replied, sounding somewhat depressed. "I just don't feel like being alone with two couples; it makes me feel bad." "But these are people you know and like quite well," I reminded her. With an impatient sigh, "I know, I know; that's not the point." "What is?" I wanted to know. "It's just uncomfortable, that's all, and I don't want to do it. Please understand," she pleaded. "I do,"

I assured her, "but you have to understand, too, that these feelings of yours put barriers in our friendship that don't have anything to do with us. Nobody who will be here tonight would give a thought to your being alone; they'd just enjoy seeing you again." Quietly, "I know. I'm not blaming you; it's me."

In fact, there's no one to blame. What she needed from me just then was a few hours of my time with her alone; what I could offer at the moment was a social event. It happens that way between any two friends sometimes. For whatever the reason, we cannot give a friend something we know she or he wants, so we offer a compromise that may be less than satisfactory to everyone concerned.

Between singles and marrieds, however, the friendship generally is dominated by such compromises, with the needs and rhythms of the married couple almost always given first consideration—a fact that singles often protest. But such is the balance of power and need in these friendships that the protest generally is a silent one—uttered to other single friends who will understand, but rarely to the married ones. A fifty-five-year-old friend, divorced for ten years, who read these pages before publication, wrote to me saying:

> A friendship with a couple takes a special kind of—I don't know what to call it; not effort, maybe self-discipline or control—from a single person. One has to learn never to speak in terms of obligation, to deal with envy, to keep gratitude within bounds, to lower expectations, to walk a very fine and delicate line so that you're never intrusive, etc., etc.
>
> It has occurred to me recently that a good many of my relationships with married people—all of them wonderfully generous and kind in their behavior toward me—are in fact quite empty. We talk about *their* lives and *their* interests, but almost never about the things that are important in my life—almost as though it's an embarrassment to them that someone roughly in their socioeconomic class and age group can live so differently and have such different concerns.
>
> Second-time-singlehood (and maybe "never marriedhood" too)

> involves a kind of adolescent behavior. (Will he call; won't he call? Does he really like me? What did he mean when he said . . . ?) Settled couples tend to find this age-inappropriate. It is, of course. But singles who persist in their old age-appropriate, marriage-appropriate behavior just grow old and die.

The gap between marrieds and singles, it seems to me, is an inevitable one, given that their major daily concerns can be so different. Single people complain that married friends seem to have little real interest in or understanding of single life, whether the pleasures or the problems. And although there's truth in this charge, the issue, I believe, is not so much what married friends say or do but the sense singles have that the power in the relationship lies with those who are married, that it is they who define both the limits and the possibilities in the friendship, they who, in essence, call the tune. Summing up our discussion about her relations with married friends, a forty-one-year-old divorcée said with some bitterness:

> Let's face it, everyone expects a single person to be more flexible and accepting. [*Sarcastically*] After all, there's only one of us and two of them. So if they want to dance, you dance; if not, too bad.

Yet from some married people, especially women, I heard similar complaints about feeling out of control in a relationship with single friends who seem only to have time for them when there is no romantic interest in sight. Several told of feeling used by single friends who move in and out of their lives with the waxing and waning of their romantic attachments. But even when this is not an issue, married women sometimes talked of feeling neglected by single friends, as these words from a thirty-three-year-old woman tell us:

> Sue and I used to be best friends, and I still care for her a lot. But I don't see her very much anymore. Since her divorce about four years ago, she's gotten a whole new set of single friends, and she doesn't have time for me anymore.

On her side, Sue had this to say:

> It's funny, I don't see so much of Jackie anymore but I still think of her as my best friend. [*Then correcting herself*] Well, maybe the truth is that she's my oldest friend and there are a lot of ties from the past there. I know she feels bad sometimes that I don't spend more time with her, but it isn't just with her; it's with them. I mean, most of the time it means I go over there for the evening, so I don't have a visit with my best friend, Jackie, but with her husband and whatever kids happen to be around. Her husband begins to look bored and I begin to feel guilty and unwelcome, so, well [*her words trailing off*] . . . What can I say?

"Then it's your discomfort at spending time with her in her family that keeps you from seeing more of her?" I asked, wanting to clarify just what she was saying.

> Well, no, that's only part of it. I used to think I'd see more of her if we could meet somewhere outside her house. But now I actually don't even think that's it. I feel a little guilty saying this, but the truth is, our lives are so different now. When I was married, either one of us would call to make arrangements for the two couples to do something. Now, if I want to go to a movie or a play on the weekend, I can't just call her up and say, "What are you doing on Friday night?" So we don't ever get together spontaneously, like I can with my single friends.
>
> [*Sitting silently for a few moments*] I think there's something even more than all of that. Let's see, how can I say it? Being single when you're a grownup is a whole new experience that only another single person really understands. Like, if I'm having some man trouble in my life, it's easier to talk to another woman who's in the same position. I don't mean that Jackie doesn't listen or care. She does. But she can't share the experience with me like a single friend can.

"Our lives are so different now . . . She can't share the experience with me." These were sentiments I heard often from single adults as they talked about the muting of their friendships with married friends. Sometimes the words are said with sadness, as they become reminders of the loss not just of a friend but of a whole way of life. Sometimes they're said with a tone that suggests they're simply a neutral statement of fact. However they're expressed, they tell us very clearly how deeply such changes in our lives affect how we relate to old friends, how they relate to us, and who our new friends will be.

One thirty-nine-year-old supervisor at the telephone company who had plenty of experience with these shifts in his life, having been married and divorced twice, and also having just ended a relationship in which he had lived with a woman for three years, sighed as he answered my questions about whether his friendships changed each time he went from coupled to single:

> Sure, I think so. I think generally when you're a couple, you want to see couples, and when you're a single, you want to see singles. Nobody likes it when they feel like you've skipped out on them. But what are you going to do? It's more comfortable to be with people who are in the same boat, and you have more in common. Like right now, I'm dating again and running around and all that. You can't hang out with couples when that's what your life's about.

The sense that friends lose their individuality once they enter a couple relationship, that the boundaries of the couple exclude them, that social behavior can change quite radically and in unexpected ways—these are some of the complaints singles have about coupled friends. Add to this the real changes in their lives when people go from singles to couples, or from couples back to singles again, and it's no surprise that single men and women both talked often and forcefully of the greater comfort and ease in being with others like themselves than with their married friends.

At the same time, there's the pain and anger of the loss or attenuation of relationships with old and valued friends. Those who have never married may find it distressing because, never having had the experience, it's difficult to understand fully how marriage can restrain people's choices about what they do, where they go, whom they see. Those who get divorced are already suffering a sense of loss and failure with the breakup of the family—a loss that's compounded when friendships decline at the same time. So they complain about feeling rejected and abandoned by old married friends. And although there's undoubtedly much reality to their grievances, until it is called to their attention in one way or another, single people often fail to notice the part they play in creating the distance between themselves and their friends of a former life.

Whether single or married, however, friends continue to have a central role in the adjustments we must make along the way of life, supporting us in learning about new ways of living, encouraging our attempts to find new ways of being. It is precisely because friends participate so closely with us in these life tasks that they change and shift as we move from singles to couples and back again.

7

On Marriage and Friendship

While satisfying some important needs, coupled social life is not enough. Thus by the late twenties or early thirties, when the first anxious years of marriage and childbearing are past, same-sex friendships come into their own again.[1] Although the interest men and women show in developing *intimate* friendships may differ, for both of them, life in a coupled world can begin to erode their sense of their own individuality.

For all of us, the "we" that is so commonly an expression of married life has both its positive side and its negative. To be "we" instead of "me" can be comforting, of course. It touches upon ancient needs and archaic experiences. To be "we" once again allays our fears that loneliness and isolation will be forever ours. Paradoxically, however, the very "we-ness" that consoles and reassures us also raises our anxieties that we will lose ourselves within it.

These are difficult issues for most people to talk about, partly because our conflict between separation and unity—between maintaining the boundaries of self against the wish to give ourselves over to another—so often remains outside of consciousness.[2] We know only that we plunge eagerly into a relationship one moment and withdraw in anxiety the next, that we long for closeness and connection with another and can feel unaccountably uncomfortable when we get it. Yet with all the difficulty of grasping and articulating such feelings, some people were able to speak about the ways in which friends served their marriage positively by alleviating their fears of the loss of a separate identity—none more gracefully than this forty-four-year-old man, a photographer in a ten-year second marriage:

> When I'm married and mostly concerned with family issues, my friendships are very much what I would call augmenting relationships. It's a way I get a whole variety of things that aren't possible in the marriage. There's also no question that it's a way I maintain an independent sense of myself also. These are friendships that are primarily mine and I don't want them shared.
>
> I suppose it's not surprising that I have several friendships with men my wife doesn't particularly like. We have arguments about these friends sometimes because she wants me not to like them also. So maybe in that sense you could say they cause some strain in the marriage. But mostly they've added a certain kind of boundary between us which I absolutely need so I won't feel swallowed up in couplehood. Actually, I think I rather like that she doesn't like these people. It absolutely assures that the friendship will be maintained independent of her and our marriage.

The friendships we form separate from the couple, then, remind us of our own identity, enabling us to retain the "I" without getting lost in the "we." But given the traditions of marriage and family, retaining a sense of individuality is a more difficult issue for a woman than for a man—one of the core issues that gave the modern feminist movement its wide appeal.

Although close personal friendships may be important to a man for other reasons, traditionally he hasn't needed them to affirm self in quite the same way a woman has because marriage doesn't strip him so profoundly of a personal identity. But until very recently, a woman almost always gave up her name, her job, her aspirations for herself—parts of life and self that help to place us in the world, to validate our identity, to confirm us as individuals who are separate and unique from any other.

Even in the face of the changes in modern family life, most

women who marry still take a man's name, mute their own dreams to nurture his. For a woman, therefore, intimate friendships with other women become important once again, at least partly because, while they acknowledge her in the *role* of Mrs. John Jones, it is in these relationships that she is also most likely to recover the parts of herself that once identified Mary Smith. As one thirty-two-year-old mother of two children, who has worked intermittently at various office jobs during the eight years of her marriage, said:

> When I'm with my friends there's a chance to remember things I forget at home—like that I have a good sense of humor and can be very funny. Between the kids and work and all, it can get so damn tense at home sometimes that I think Tom and I both forget. Unfortunately, I don't have nearly enough time to see my friends as much as I want to. But when I do, part of the relief of it is that I can get to be something besides Tom's wife and the kids' mother. They remind me that I was once a pretty smart and fun-loving person.
>
> [*A reflective pause*] Don't misunderstand me; Tom and I can have fun together too. But it's different because there's all this other stuff between us—all the responsibilities and what we expect from each other, things like that.

With friends, the expectations are more moderate while, at the same time, the norms surrounding friendship permit physical distance and psychological separation—indeed, at various times, require both for the maintenance of the relationship. Thus friends provide the safety within which intimacy can occur without the violation of self, as these words from a forty-six-year-old woman, married twenty-one years, show:

> If things get sticky with friends, you can bow out for a while. You don't call for a week or so, and nobody notices. Or if they do, you have a handy excuse. You can't do that with a husband because you're there in the same house all the time. I can tell a close friend something that's bothersome but it doesn't affect her, so it's no big

deal. But with my husband, when I tell him I'm not feeling good about something, he behaves as if I'm blaming him, like he's done something wrong by not making me some kind of a happy idiot.

[*Stopping to correct herself*] No, that's not fair. But he *does* want to be reassured that I'm okay so he'll feel okay. Sometimes it gets so mushy between us that I'm not sure whether what I'm thinking is mine or his. When those kinds of feelings get a good hold on me, I run off to my friends for consolation—you know, to get back on my own ground.

It isn't just the rules that structure relations in marriage that are responsible for a woman's difficulty in retaining the integrity of the self she has built over the years. Rather it's the way these rules come together with her own deeply felt needs for emotional connection that does the trick.

When a woman begins to feel anxious about the loss of self—sometimes because of the terms of the relationship with a man, sometimes because of her own internal wish to disintegrate the boundaries between them, most often because of a combination of the two—she'll make some moves to create distance. But then she finds herself in a bind. She still craves the connection she has just given up, yet her fears of merger with him make this one unsafe. So she turns to a friend with whom the boundaries are clearer and fusion less likely.

For a man, it's different. For all the reasons I have already discussed, he has fewer problems with maintaining his boundaries and less immediately felt need for the kind of intimacy his wife seeks so insistently. Therefore, once he marries, he's content to have friendships that are, as the man above said, "augmenting relationships"—friendships with people whose conversation and companionship he enjoys. For the more intimate moments, for the emotional support he needs and wants, he looks to his wife.[3]

For a woman, relating to a woman friend seems, in some important ways, like relating to self—a continuation of her early identification with mother. Indeed, this is part of what makes intimate friendships with other women so compelling. For a man, the *idea* of intimacy in a relationship is also connected to a woman and for essentially the same reasons. Therefore, it's to a woman he most naturally turns as he seeks gratification of his needs for a close connection with another.

I am not arguing that women don't value intimate relations with men, only that what happens between them is quite different from the kind of connection two women make. Nor am I saying that men do not also share a deep and important bond with each other, only that it doesn't rest in so early and primitive a place inside them.

Most of the men I met seemed to take the lack of intimate friendships in their own lives quite calmly, insisting that they didn't notice it until it was called to their attention, that the companionship and stimulation they get from other men meets their needs quite nicely. Once it was brought up for discussion, these men said simply that they had "plenty of company at work," see "as many people as [they] need," find "enough closeness" in their relations with their wives. Although they were quite aware of the disparity between themselves and their wives in this realm—"I don't have friends like she does"—few exhibited any feelings about it—"I never felt the need."

Some men, however, did express the wish that their friendships were different, saying they were jealous of their wives' ability to form such close and sustaining relationships. A thirty-seven-year-old businessman, married fourteen years, spoke about the differences between his friendships and his wife's, lamenting the lack of intimacy in his relationships while also acknowledging his pleasure in some of their typically male qualities.

> When I see how full Natalie's life is compared to mine, I don't like it. I sometimes feel a little jealous of the ease with which she, and a lot of other women I see, seem to be able to make friends. There are men I talk to—guys I have lunch with at work, or the men I

> play cards with, or other men I know. But it's either shop talk or horsing around, not like the things I hear Nat talking to her women friends about.
>
> Don't get me wrong. I don't mind talking about work; I like it. I like the kind of easy banter that goes on between men; it's comfortable and fun. But I can't imagine calling anybody up and having a ten-minute conversation with him, except if it's about work, let alone the hours Nat and her friends spend on the phone.

"Are you saying you'd like to be able to do that?" I asked. Smiling, he replied:

> No, not exactly. I hate the damn phone. I think what I mean is I'd like to have that kind of ease of expressing what's inside me. And also I'd like to have a couple of friends like that who I could really talk to. But it just doesn't happen with men.

Others disparaged their wives' friendships with disdain, dismissing them as trivial and meaningless. But the very heat with which these men spoke suggests they have feelings that belie their words.

"If I live to be a hundred, I'll never be able to figure out what the hell they talk about so much."

"Have you ever listened to two women gabbing for hours? Garbage, plain garbage!"

"Jesus, I get pissed when she gets on the phone for an hour rattling about *nothing.*"

"Last night I went to a meeting and left her sitting on the couch talking to a friend. And would you believe it, three hours later, they're still there talking? Yeah, yeah, I've seen it before, but it always sets me off. What do women talk about so much?"

"What do women talk about so much?" Not just a question or a complaint, but a cry born of feelings that arise unbidden out of their unremembered but painful past—the time when the exclusive relationship with mother was disrupted. When a man sees a loved woman's involvement with another, it raises for him fears that his wife, like his mother, is another woman whose steadfastness cannot be trusted. Therefore, he's likely to find himself unaccountably uncomfortable, angry, jealous. But since these feelings can seem so irrational even to him, he distorts them into the kind of angry mockery of women and their relationships that men so commonly express.

In fact, what a man wants in moments such as these is the reassurance that another loss is not to be his. He wants her to come close, to stand by, to be available without distraction, as these words from a thirty-six-year-old building contractor, married eight years, tell:

> I come home after a hard day's work and I'm ready to sit and relax. All I want is for her to come sit by me, nice and quiet. And what does she do? She goes and calls up a friend.

He wants, in sum, the mother whose presence alone was enough to soothe and warm him. And as with her, he wants it all to happen wordlessly—another mother who will intuit his need, his fear, his loneliness. Only then can he recreate the feelings of that original bond, even if only for a moment or an hour. But a woman wants to talk.

There is perhaps nothing more symbolic of this difference between them than the telephone and the way they each use it. Few men have the kind of long conversations on the phone that so engage most women. For a man, the telephone is an instrument of communication, something to reach for to make or confirm some arrangement, to pass on a message. When I talked with men about this, some said that after being plagued by the phone all day at work, they considered it an enemy by the time they came home at night.

> I get as much of the damn phone as I can stand all day long. It's one interruption after the other until I want to rip it out of the wall. When I have something on deadline—an important report I have to turn out or something like that—I'll have to get away from the office to get it done because of the phone.

A familiar story. But men who never touch the phone during the workday seem to be equally resistant to it at night. And women who spend many working hours on the telephone may complain about its intrusions during the day but, nevertheless, have lengthy telephone conversations in the evening. For them, the phone is more than an instrument through which to pass information. It's a welcome social tool, an opportunity for a visit with a friend when none other is possible. For them, a phone call is a substitute for the face-to-face encounter that time or distance will not permit, enabling friends to sustain a close connection even when they can't see each other as much as they would wish. A thirty-five-year-old nurse, married twelve years, put it this way:

> My life's so busy that I don't have time to see my friends nearly as much as I really want to, which is why we talk on the phone so much. That's the way we keep up with each other's lives, you know, how we know what's going on. We do a lot of problem solving on the phone too. If we waited to see each other, the problems would either be gone or so big you wouldn't know where to grab hold.

It's not just the need to keep in touch with friends that motivates these phone conversations between women, however. They're prompted also by the lack of verbal interaction with their men—by their need for some kind of reciprocal sharing of self and experience with another in the face of a man's wish "for her to come sit by me, nice and quiet." With a sigh of resignation, the same woman explained:

> My being on the phone at night makes problems, I know it does. Larry just hates it. Most of the time he keeps quiet, but sometimes there's a big blowup about it. Then we have one of those stupid fights where we both holler dumb things at each other.
>
> Even though I usually only say it when I get mad like that, I really think I wouldn't talk on the phone so much when he's around if he'd talk to me. But he doesn't; he's content just to sit

> quietly, maybe reading or watching TV or something. If I try to talk to him, you know, to find out what's going on with him, he doesn't really say much. Even if I tell him something about the kids or some problem I've been thinking about, he'll listen, but it doesn't turn into a conversation the way it does with a woman friend. So after a while, I begin to feel kind of lonely, and I go make a call, or someone calls me and I'm glad for the chance to talk.

This is another major reason why women's friendships are so important to them, why so many women insist that, rather than being a strain on the marriage, their friendships are an important source of support for it. Woman after woman told of the ways in which friends fill the gaps the marriage relationship leaves, allowing the wife to appreciate those things the husband can give rather than to focus on those he can't.

"I often use my friends and the safety and closeness I feel with them to work out problems or lacks in my marriage."

"There have been times when I haven't felt particularly good or safe in my marriage, when my friends have come to the rescue. Being able to turn to them and test out what I really feel has been a life-saver—or maybe I should say a marriage-saver."

"I don't think any marriage could survive, or at least any one I could be in, without good friends."

"Being able to go off and talk to one of my women friends gives me a perspective so that I don't have to niggle away at Martin for the things he and I don't do so well together."

"It isn't even anything my friends say to me when we talk about personal things that helps. I just come away realizing that I'm lucky I have other people who understand me."

"Just like there isn't a perfect friend, there isn't a perfect husband or lover. That's why people need both, and if they don't have them, there's going to be trouble."

The expression of these sentiments tells us that, for women at least, friends outside the marriage facilitate the acceptance of the limits inside it—the limits that, in one way or another, every relationship will reach. It's not the recognition of these limits, not the turning outward to fill the gaps with friends, that's a threat to a marriage. Rather it's the persistent efforts to transcend all limits, the insistence that our ideal of perfect communion can and will be met, that can be so damaging. One fifty-four-year-old woman in a thirty-year marriage summed it up neatly:

> No two people can be everything for each other, nor should they be, nor should we have such impossible expectations. Friendship is really a way to get some of the other things that you don't get from the particular person you love and married. If I'm satisfied in a variety of different places, like with my work and my friends, then if Ben's spaced out and can't be there for me, it isn't a big deal. If I waited breathlessly for him to come home and didn't have my work and my friends, well [*her words trailing off*] . . .

Work and friends—two central parts of life, each given equal weight. But here we see again how the early experiences in the family and the developmental tasks boys and girls each must undertake there continue to make themselves felt later in life.

It's not the time work and family demand that interferes with friendship, as so many men claim. And it's certain that men don't find total satisfaction in their relations with their wives any more than women do with their husbands. But for men, the whole constellation of friends, family and work is experienced very differently than for most women. Among women, for whom relationships are never far from center stage, friends are necessary even when work life is important and gratifying. Among men, for whom work lies at the heart of life, even of their very identity, relationships are of secondary concern.[4]

This is one place where both age and environment make some small difference. Men under forty, who also live in those urban centers where they are apt to have been most heavily influenced by the feminist ferment of recent years, are more likely than other men to make and maintain close friendships after marriage. But even among this group, there were surprisingly few such friendships—less than one-fifth of these men giving evidence of friends who held an important place in their emotional lives.

For women, the lack of friends in their men's lives is often a mixed blessing. On the one hand, women complain about this, feel burdened by a man's emotional dependence, which seems to rest so heavily on them.

"It's damn hard knowing that there's no one else he ever really talks to. I'm all he's got."

"I'm the only person he would ever reveal himself to at all, which leaves me feeling a tremendous responsibility to him."

"You don't know how I wish he had the kind of experience with friends that I have. Then my relationships with my close friends wouldn't bother him so much."

"Sometimes I don't mind, but other times it feels like such a damn burden to have him so dependent on me socially and emotionally."

"I'll bet he told you he has friends when you interviewed him. Believe me, he doesn't—at least not anybody he talks to about anything. I sure wish he did so I wouldn't be the only one."

With all their complaints, however, there's also something reassuring for a woman to know that she's the singular source of emotional support in her husband's life. By furnishing this kind of emotional sustenance, by providing him with the one place where he can be at least somewhat free of the emotional chains inside him, she gives him the one thing he cannot give himself. A man can buy housekeeping services, can find sex fairly easily these days, can get certain kinds of companionship from another man. But the kind of social and emotional service I have been speaking of here, he can usually allow only from a wife or a lover. In a world where a woman is so much less powerful in a relationship than a man, this equalizes things a little, helps her to feel stronger and safer.

It's not surprising, therefore, that in the few instances where a man had a close friend with whom he had an important emotional tie, his wife was not unequivocally pleased about the relationship, even when she had such friends of her own. It's not just ordinary jealousy I saw, although that certainly was there. Rather these women felt displaced, as if their rightful place had been usurped. A thirty-two-year-old woman spoke with painful honesty about the feelings she was having now that her husband had the friend she had been urging on him for some time.

> Sometimes I think there's something the matter with me. I go out with friends and it's okay; Bruce hardly ever complains. And when he does, I get pissed, like I don't want him interfering with my freedom and my friendships. But he recently got close to a man, and I find myself resenting it when they go off and do things together. For a long time, I've nagged him about getting some friends of his own, and now that he has, I feel [*groping for the right words*] not exactly jealous, but something like it. Maybe it's just that I'm used to being his be-all and end-all, and I guess I didn't dislike that as much as I thought I did.

It should be clear: The same women who express such doubts usually also are genuinely glad when their husband makes a friend. They feel freer, less burdened, less bound to be present and available all the time, less guilty about the time and energy spent in maintaining their own friendships, reassured about the social capability and desirability of their husband. But this new development is not simply the answer to a woman's prayers. It also presents a problem that must be met and mastered—quite a different one from the early years when a woman sought to break a man's ties to his friends and fix his dependency in the marriage.

In the intervening years, the same man may have become almost wholly dependent on his wife for the social and emotional balance in his life. When he begins to develop friendships with other men again, it means a shift in the established ways of being in the family that raises for his wife anxieties about her place in his life, about what the new balance will be. Thus she may be honestly pleased with the change while also being unable to appreciate it fully until a new equilibrium comes to pass that assuages her concerns.

It's another of those paradoxes of family life. So long as men have more power, status and prestige than women in the world outside, women will be ambivalent at best about giving up those areas of control that traditionally have been theirs inside the family. So long as a man of forty is seen as a desirable "commodity," and a woman of the same age as "over the hill," women will be uneasy when their men stray from the home.

Still, since men are so much less liable to have close friendships than women, it's men who are more subject to jealousy over the friendships their wives form—jealousy that stirs feelings of sometimes agonizing intensity and creates dangerous conflict and confusion for both the marriage and the individuals in it. If friends are abandoned in an attempt to palliate these anxieties, it is not only the friendship that suffers but the marriage as well. For while we may give such a "gift" to a mate, the emotional price to the couple relationship can be very high. A forty-nine-year-old woman, married twenty-seven years, talked about the difficulties when, in the early years of her marriage, she and her husband were in conflict over her friendships:

> When we were first married, Michael was very jealous of my friends. He resented the people I was really close to, and, at first, I tried to be accommodating about it. But it nearly ruined our marriage because I was always furious with him because he certainly couldn't be *all* the things I wanted and needed. Those were our hard years, until we both learned what marriage is about and what you can really reasonably expect from another human being.

Few people today would argue with the notion that friends outside the marriage take some of the heat off inside. But most also know that the relationship between the two is not always benign. As I moved about, therefore, I heard stories of the man who ran off with his friend's wife; of the woman who had an affair with her friend's husband; of the friend who encouraged the breakup of a marriage, consciously or unconsciously advocating for divorce as a way of living out his or her own unfulfilled wishes vicariously.

Most of the time, however, a friend's intervention in our lives is not that direct. Rather the influence friends exert is connected much more to the depth of our identification with them than to any action they take, advice they give, or words they speak. It's no secret, for example, that in the first flush of the women's movement, large numbers of women were able to leave unsatisfactory marriages—not because anyone told them to or brainwashed them, as many among feminism's opponents have complained, but because of the support for their grievances they found among their feminist friends.

Among the people I met, some spoke of how important friendships in their lives supported their marriage at one time and facilitated their divorce at a later moment. It wasn't so much that these friends did or said anything different at different times. Rather it was how they lived their own lives, what kind of model for living—or, more accurately, for marriage or divorce—they provided. This story, told by a woman now forty-five and divorced seven years, is a good example:

> I don't know when I would have been able to leave my marriage if it weren't for my relationship with my best friend, Joyce. [*A brief pause*] Hmmm, when I said that, I almost immediately thought, "No, that's not quite right." I mean, it's right, but it's not all because she was also what allowed the marriage to continue, maybe a lot longer than it should have. I always knew there were things that were unsatisfactory for me in that marriage. But with Joyce in my life, it wasn't necessary to put all those demands on him. She was my whole emotional world during that period—she and my children, of course.
>
> We were so close. We both had young children then, and nei-

> ther of us was working. So we saw each other or talked every day. We really were a support network for each other. We were both unhappily married, and we weren't sure what we were going to do about it, if anything at all. Neither of us thought we had the courage to do something about it, in fact.
>
> Then she met this man, and it became clearer and clearer to both of us that she was getting ready to leave her husband. It was like a model for me of what was possible and, for the first time, I knew that I could leave too. It took a little while, but I did it. When I look back, I wonder what would have happened if she hadn't taken that turn. It was as if she gave me permission to get divorced even though, of course, nothing like that was ever said.

The identification between these two women was a factor, of course. But so was the historical moment through which they were living. When the norms and values that traditionally have surrounded marriage and the family are called into question at the same time that we put a premium on individual growth, a friend's divorce may give permission to seek individual fulfillment at the expense of the marriage.

Had they lived in another era, both these women might well have accommodated to their discontents. For when divorce made women social pariahs, they were much less likely to take the step. Today they'll have plenty of friends to keep them company. But for this, we cannot blame their friends. They are not the cause of the present state of marriage; they are simply reflectors of the current social reality.

All this notwithstanding, by and large, friends serve both marriage and the individual well. In relation to the marriage, they fill the gaps that a mate, no matter how loving and loved, cannot fill. In relation to the individual, friends support a much needed sense of separateness, help each person to retain an independent sense of self and identity.

When we first marry, we eagerly seek out others who share our social role and circumstance because they help to affirm that part of our self and our life, to validate our connection to our new roles as wife and husband. Soon after, however, we begin to look also for people who see the individual in us, who encourage the appearance of a self-in-the-world who lives beyond the boundaries of the self-in-the-role. We need both: Our individual friends tend to support our unique personal identity; our couple friends buttress the twosome, the "we" rather than the "I." Together, these friends serve to validate those parts of self that spill over the confines of the role of husband or wife *and* also provide yet another tie to bind us to the marriage itself.

Women and Men as Friends

Mind, Body and Emotion

The history of conquest and seduction that has for so long dominated relations between women and men is not easily left behind.[1] Therefore, when I asked about their friendships with the opposite sex, most people's thoughts turned quickly to the ways in which sex, whether acted on or not, both gives the relationship a special charge and also creates difficulties that are not easily overcome.[2] These words from a thirty-four-year-old single man, a computer scientist, tell graphically how the traditional postures of men and women inhibit friendship between them.

> The whole idea of friendship with women as opposed to a sexual relationship is a puzzle. It's not codified; you don't know what the rules are. And it's not something that's celebrated as any ideal in movies or books or anything.
>
> How do you get to be friends with a woman and not have to come on in any way? Friendship is almost in opposition to the love relationship game, which is what makes it so hard for men and women to be really good friends. If you're a friend you don't have to use any kind of a line, or play any kind of a role, or act some part that's not really you just to score with a woman.

Sometimes people said they "had to get sex out of the way" in order to consolidate a friendship in a relationship where they knew or suspected from the start that a romance wouldn't work. This explains, I believe, why women and men will often report a brief sexual adventure as a prelude to a friendship. Once the tensions of unexplored sex are behind them, and they have decided together that the complications of a sexual relationship are not worth the risk to the friendship, they are freed from the strains that so often inhibit friendship between men and women.[3]

Although we may sometimes abhor these familiar interactions between men and women, they also carry certain meanings that we find reassuring to our sense of ourselves and our desirability. Therefore, giving up the attempt to "score" or ignoring the sexual charge that exists for one or the other or both often doesn't work very well either. For when we do, we may find ourselves in what this thirty-two-year-old single woman, a middle manager in a large corporation, described as a situation "you can't really win."

> I'd like to have friendships with men, but I don't seem to be able to pull it off very well. If you get sexually involved, it ruins whatever friendship was possible, and if you don't, there's all that gaminess that goes on. In my experience, it's a problem whatever you do or [*making a face to emphasize the irony of her words*] don't do.
>
> I used to be friends with this guy who never made any kind of a sexual overture, and I didn't exactly love that either. It made me feel unattractive and undesirable. It wasn't even so much that I wanted to go to bed with him, but I wanted him to want to.

Even in this free and enlightened sexual age, only a few people, much more often men than women, said they could mix sex and friendship easily. One twenty-six-year-old woman, an accounting clerk, distinguished between what she called "friendly, almost platonic, sex," which caused no problems in a friendship for her, and "romantic sex," which meant trouble:

> It's no big deal for me to have sex with one of my men friends when I need some comfort or I'm just plain horny. It fulfills a

need, almost like an appetite or a hunger, I guess, and it's comforting if I'm feeling low or something like that. But that's just friendly, almost platonic, sex—nothing romantic about it. Now when there's a guy I have some romantic interest in, that's romantic sex. Then I can't have that kind of easy sex because I want something else, and if I can't get it, it ruins the relationship.

Most people, however, insist that introducing sex into a friendship is an almost sure way to raise irreconcilable conflicts, that even when a couple start out believing "friendly sex" won't change anything between them, they're due for a surprise.

"Once you get sex involved, there's no way out without someone getting hurt."

"I don't think sex just inhibits friendship; it overpowers it and pushes it out."

"A woman's your friend and it's fine. Then you go to bed together and all of a sudden she starts wanting something else."

"Sex and friendship? Not a chance! Sex makes people possessive, which is exactly what friendships can't tolerate."

"In my experience, and watching it with others, having a sexual relationship with someone seems most often to preclude the best part of friendship—I mean the kind of trust and good will that goes with a good friendship."

"It makes a mess because if you act on the sexual pull, it's almost surely going to mean the end of the friendship, and then you're probably going to be stuck with nothing, no lover and no friend—at least for a long time, until everybody's feelings get put back together again."

Many people today, of course, do tell of friendships with ex-lovers, but almost always the transition is a long and painful one, the hiatus in the relationship filled with hurt and anger. For sex stirs longings in us that are not easily stilled—longings that bring to the fore the jealousy and possessiveness, the ambivalence and fears, about which men and women complain.

Undoubtedly the social proscriptions around sexual expression are partly responsible for the feelings unloosed by a sexual relationship. A society's norms around sex and sexuality are so deeply internalized that they not only mold our behavior but make themselves felt in the experience of our own sexuality as well. We may tell ourselves that it's time to change our sexual ways, that other cultures don't invest sex with such tremendous emotional significance as ours does. But such intellectual exhortations will not still the conflicts that arise when we are *acting* in new ways yet with *feelings* that reflect the old ones.

So, for example, although many women scoff at the old sexual conventions, the prohibition against sex without love is not wholly inoperative—consciously for some, less so for others.[4] It's not unusual, therefore, for a woman to start a sexual relationship knowing she's not in love, only to get lost in fantasies of love, marriage and forever by the time she has spent a couple of nights with a man, as this from a twenty-nine-year-old professional woman shows:

> Getting involved sexually makes me a little crazy. All of a sudden I find myself turning this guy I'm sleeping with into some kind of paragon of manhood that I can't live without. I just lose it—my good sense, I mean, that really knows he's not for me and I'm not in love with him.

But the cultural mandates around sexuality and the way they affect us can only partly explain the difficulties most people have when they try to mix sex and friendship. For most of us, the sexual encounter taps layers of feelings that, in adult life, are unique to it—feelings that are roused, at least in part, by the actual blurring of boundaries that takes place only in sex. Whether in a man or a woman, this fusion seems to promise to fulfill our most archaic and infantile fantasies, exposing in us a set of needs and longings for union with another that are antithetical to a friendship. For sex requires the merging of two people—not just physically but psychologically as well—where friendship rests on respect for their separateness.

In coming together sexually, our bodies are merged, preparing the way for the psychological disintegration of the boundaries that normally separate us, which, in turn, permits the experience of unity with another again. We go to bed, have sex, and paradoxically, the better it is, the more difficult the separation, the harder it is to understand the need for it—feelings that become much more acute with a loved friend than with a stranger.

In our head, we remind ourselves that this is *just* a friend, that we have no right to these feelings. But the heart has other concerns. Suddenly, friend becomes someone else—the cruel depriver, the purveyor of the pain of unfilled longings. Suddenly, we are no longer with a friend, but with a representation of every person who ever left us with needs unmet.

This is the source of the greedy jealousy that's so often a part of a sexual relationship, the source, too, of the possessiveness and the demand for exclusivity it generates. Just as we once sought exclusive possession of our mother, we now seek the same in any relationship that replays that early experience. When it fails the fantasy, as any adult relationship must, an infantile rage can overwhelm the rational adult, leaving the relationship in shreds.

It's different for men and for women, of course, as different as were their early developmental experiences in the family. For a man, the split between sex and emotion, together with the boundaries he developed in childhood, help him to maintain some distance from his inner emotional experience, help also to make the fear of merging with another less compelling for him than for the woman who shares his bed.

But at the same time, sex is often the one place where a man's emotional control is shaken—where he can contact and express his deeper feeling states, where the boundary between self and other will not always hold firm. Thus, while he finds pleasure and comfort in the surrender to a woman's body, in being nourished there once again, somewhere inside him lives also the memory of the betrayal that cast him out of that warmth. So he becomes fearful, seeking to firm up the boundaries once again, to create some distance that will keep him safe. Talking about the anxieties sex can awaken in him, a forty-one-year-old printer said:

> Much as I love sex, it raises a barrier for me. Somehow the issue of trust is always there—I mean, whether I can trust a woman with all that vulnerability that comes out when you're sexual. [*With a toss of his head and a smile*] It's not like I have a choice; I'm straight as an arrow. But it's one big reason a friendship can't make it for me if it turns sexual.

For a woman, too, sex brings a mix of delight and fear that bodes ill for a friendship. For her, there's great pleasure in the merger that's experienced in sex, deep satisfaction in this union with another. At the same time, the very intensity of her feelings stimulates the fear that her joy in the oneness will be so great as to sweep away her hard-won ability to remain a distinct and separate person. A forty-year-old divorced woman, the manager of a specialty clothing shop, talked about just these fears:

> Once a relationship becomes sexual, I'm inclined to give too much away. I get all those longings for someone who'll be there forever and all that stuff. It becomes dangerous to—how can I say it?—to my wholeness. And since most of those relationships don't work out anyway, why would I ruin a good friendship? For what?

Certainly there are women today who manage a sexual relationship without kindling fantasies of "forever and all that stuff." Over the years, I have met such women, have interviewed them in one or another research project, have seen them in my clinical practice. But they are far less prevalent than the behavior we see would lead us to expect. For to bring the behavior and feelings into harmony, we must internalize some new and expanded sense of our own sexuality, which means also that we will come into contact with a new and different sense of that very important part of self. It's precisely because our sense of self and our sexuality are not readily separable that the internal changes come so slowly.

Not surprisingly, friendships across the gender line are much less common among couples, married or not, than among singles,[5] since the jealousy and possessiveness that so often marks a sexual relationship reaches its zenith among those who are living a coupled life.[6] Here again, however, class makes a difference not only in the frequency of cross-sex friendships among those who are coupled, but also in whether it's likely to be a matter that's up for discussion or settled by fiat. Thus while friendship between men and women who are married and/or living together in a committed relationship is not common in any class—only 22 percent of the men and 16 percent of the women I interviewed claimed such friendships—most of them, by far, existed among the college-educated middle class.[7]

Many of these friendships start at work where white-collar workers and professionals are much more likely than their working-class counterparts to have colleagues of the opposite sex. Many of them also are confined to what little free time the work setting permits—to coffee or lunch, sometimes a drink immediately after the day is done. When a cross-sex friendship moves beyond those boundaries, it's often a cause for at least some doubts and jealousies on the part of the mate. "I'd have to pay a lot of dues at home to go see a woman for dinner," said a thirty-one-year-old professional man, married six years. "It would have to be some wonderful dinner to make it worthwhile."

There are, of course, some who sustain important cross-sex friendships even after marriage. These are mostly professional people who tend to marry considerably later than others, not infrequently these days in their late twenties and well into their thirties. By the time they marry, these women and men have behind them a decade or more of living as independent adults. Therefore, they come to the marriage with a comparatively well-established set of friendships, sometimes including those of the opposite sex—relationships that are not given up easily even in the face of pressure from a mate. As one thirty-two-year-old woman, a doctor, married less than a year, said:

> I have two men friends, one from college and one who was a lover for a short while about eight years ago. Jon didn't love the idea when we first got together, but he understood that they've been in my life for a long time, and that's just the way it's going to be [*with a furrowed brow*] . . . unless they get into a relationship with a woman who has a fit about me. I don't think they'd give in, but I know enough to know you can't predict, can you?

Among working-class couples, who tend to marry soon after high school, there's little experience with adult relationships between women and men in which the sexual issues are handled with some maturity. Instead, images of relationships with the opposite sex generally remain rooted in the teen-age years when sexual games were the norm, when a boy tested his manhood by trying to "make her" and a girl played "hard to get," all the while "holding out" for the right moment to "give in." With this scenario in the background, once they marry, it's generally taken for granted that a friendship between a man and a woman is a danger that's not to be tolerated. Thus a thirty-seven-year-old husband, a machinist, snorted:

> Friends with women? You've got to be kidding. It's nothing but trouble for anybody that cares about his marriage.

His thirty-five-year-old wife, a beautician, spoke more gently, but the view she expressed was much the same:

> No, I don't have men friends. Even if I wanted to, Ray's so jealous he'd kill me. I understand how he feels, because I sure wouldn't like him to have some woman for a friend either.

Yet with all the potential for problems that sex brings to friendship, many men and women continue to seek each other out for non-romantic relationships. "What do you get out of a friendship with a man [woman] that's different from a same-sex relationship?" I asked everyone who claimed such friendships.

Women and men both agreed that, although the sexual charge could potentially confound a friendship, it also added a certain zest, a special excitement that can't be had in a same-sex friendship. Some people spoke of a flirtatious quality in the relationship, saying they valued it because it imparted a quality of vitality to the time they spent together, because it generated a spark they enjoyed.

"We both certainly know we'll never act on it, but there's still that small element of flirtatiousness that adds to the fun."

"The flirty boy-girl stuff spices up a friendship with a man and makes it kind of exciting—at least for the moment."

"You get this extra added attraction with a woman—her femaleness, which I enjoy being near. It's part of the zing in the friendship."

Others talked of the way these friendships validated their attractiveness as male or female and affirmed their femininity or masculinity.

"I don't know how to explain it. We don't exactly come on to each other, but there's a subtle knowledge that she's a woman and I'm a man that feels very good. It's reassuring—like a reminder of what's possible when I'm down."

"What can I say? When I see myself mirrored in my friend Janet's eyes, it's a pickup in a way no man can do it for me. She doesn't like or admire me as just another person but also as a man."

"When I meet a man friend and see that admiring look as I walk up, it touches something deep inside me. I walk taller and feel more feminine."

"I go to Susan for woman things and she comes to me for man things. There's something about it that feels—how should I say it?—very confirming of me and my manliness."

But here their agreement ended. Beyond these issues, men and women not only valued their friendships with each other differently, but their perceptions about the intimacy and closeness of the relationship frequently differed as well.

By and large, men seemed less ambivalent about these friendships than women did, found them more clearly satisfying. No surprise here. A man expects less than a woman in any friendship, whether with a woman or a man, and what expectations he does have are much more clearly divided according to gender stereotypes. Therefore, he's most likely to turn to another man for play and for talk of weighty affairs—work, politics, serious intellectual matters—and to look for a woman to share the softer, more emotional side of his life.

It's not always so cleanly split, of course. Some men talk quite convincingly of appreciating a woman's intellect or her ability at a certain kind of problem solving. Even in the most highly self-conscious men, however, the problems they take to a man or a woman are usually quite different. They may talk about work to both. But it's a man who is called upon to help solve the intellectual problems there, a woman to advise on the interpersonal ones. One forty-two-year-old divorced man, an executive in a large publishing house, mused thoughtfully about this gender division of labor in his friendships and finally concluded:

> In some ways, my friendships express the traditional kind of splitting where the more interior issues are shared with women and the exterior ones with men.

Over and over, men spoke about the fact that a woman's friendship provides the nurturance and intimacy not generally available in their relations with men.[8]

"Even if you talk about the same things, the conversation has a whole different focus with a woman. Talking with a woman has a more feeling quality. It's more nurturing and less defensive, less of the male-male kind of competitive quality, I would say."

"My closest friends are women because I don't have to play the male game with them. I can show my weaknesses to a woman friend and she'll be accepting, not judgmental."

Yet the very women of whom these men speak rarely share fully the man's perceptions of the relationship. About two-thirds of the women who were named by a man as a close friend disavowed that definition of the relationship. Most acknowledged the friendship but did not count it as a close or intimate one. A few even questioned the fact that they were considered a friend, preferring to think of their relationship with this particular man as more casual than the word "friend" implied to them.

Whether casual or close, most women agree that in their friendships with men, they listen and nurture. Sometimes they admit that they revel in this affirmation of their superiority over men in the emotional realm. There's a certain pride for women in the knowledge that they're better than men at relating intimately, and a sense of power in the knowledge that for this, men usually turn to them rather than to each other. But more often than not, they also complain. "I do too much of the giving in my friendships with men," they'll explain. "There's not much reciprocity," they'll fret. "He talks, I listen," they'll grumble.

As for the level of intimacy, women rarely feel their relationships with men are a match for the friendships they share with women.[9] Of all the women who spoke of friendships with men, only five put them in a class with close women friends. And all of them said of these particular men, "He's more like a woman." "His feminine side is the most highly developed of any man I've ever known." Apart from these few, even women who counted men among their close friends felt some barriers around intimacy and intensity in these relationships.

"My men friends are mostly for fun and sports, for doing

things with. We talk too, but the *real* talking is with my women friends."

"I have fun with men, and they can even be supportive and helpful about some things, but it's such a different thing from relating to women. I don't find men able to tell me the process of their thoughts, the stream of consciousness, the way they think—you know, the kind of conversation you can always get into with a woman."

"I have one man friend I love very much, but I don't relate to him like I do to a woman. I can't talk to him the same way, and when I try, I'm disappointed. Sometimes when I'm with him, I find myself getting bored. Either we're talking about him and his problems and I'm sort of like a mother or big sister, or it's all so heady and intellectualized that it's boring."

"With a woman, there's always something to chew on. You know what I mean. Something's brought up and we dissect it and look at it from all angles for hours. With a man, he goes for the solution, and that's not always what you want."

"He goes for the solution"—one of the differences between men and women that often makes conversation less than satisfactory for both of them. Even when children are each given the same set of facts about a human relationship, a boy sees a problem that needs a solution while a girl sees a process that needs understanding, as Carol Gilligan has shown persuasively.[10] In adulthood, these patterns remain much the same. A man looks to reason and logic for resolution—to a cool, dispassionate assessment of the facts. A woman wants to "dissect" and "chew"—to understand the issues underlying the facts, to figure out how the problem came to be, why Jane acted this way, Joe the other way, what everyone was thinking, feeling, wanting. It's not that the solution is unimportant or irrelevant, only that, for her, a satisfactory resolution must rest on this kind of understanding.

Sometimes their different ways of approaching an issue will lead to the same answer. When that happens, a man is likely to shake his head in wonder. "All that talk just to get where I was hours ago," he'll mutter. "If I could only get her to be logical, it all would be so much easier," he'll complain. But they miss the point. It's not that logic and an ability to appraise the facts elude a woman. Rather it's the process that brought those facts to life that seems at least as important to her as the facts themselves; and it's the process of examining their varying facets that engages her most intensely.

For a woman, the search for a solution requires understanding of the process on which an interaction rests, understanding also of how and why all the pieces fit together as they do. For a man, this style is exasperating. It's his inability or unwillingness to follow her mental path, to examine the intricacies of an interaction rather than just the facts, that provokes her irritation. "How come there's no give-and-take in a conversation with a man? Sometimes it's like trying to play tennis with no one in the other court."

"If your conversations with men aren't as emotionally satisfying as with women, and if your friendships with them aren't particularly intimate or nurturing, what do they provide?" I asked all the women who spoke this way.

Most women agreed that the very differences that trouble them in their friendships with men, the differences about which they so often complain, are also what makes these friendships of particular interest to them—at least part of the time. They miss the warmer emotional tone of their relations with women, they said, but appreciate also the cooler ambience of a friendship with a man. They talked repeatedly, and often spiritedly, of valuing the male perspective, of learning something from it that they couldn't get in their friendships with women.

"The payoff in having men for friends is that I feel that the diversity they bring to my life makes me richer."

"It adds something to my own growth to understand their outlook and try to bridge the differences."

"I use my male friends as sounding boards to get a male point of view, which is the one thing I can't get from my women friends."

Some added also that these very characteristic differences in cognitive style that often aggravate them also pique their interest, making the relationship a challenge of sorts, almost, as one woman said, "like trying to solve a puzzle or a mystery."

"I'm one with a woman. I can figure what she's thinking and feeling and why. But with a man, I have to pay a different kind of attention. I have to listen with my head, not just with my guts or my heart."

"I get a particular kind of kick out of trying to figure out how that male mind works and matching it."

"There's something different and challenging about the male intellectual style, and sometimes it fits the bill. I have kind of a love-hate relationship to that one-two-three problem-solving mode of theirs. There are times when I can't stand it, and then other times when it's exactly what I'm looking for."

Not infrequently the same woman who, moments earlier, had complained about the lack of emotional content in a friendship with a man also spoke of the relief such a relationship can bring. Talking about these contradictory feelings, a thirty-five-year-old artist and teacher summarized the conflict:

> Once we got the sexual stuff out of the way, it began to be a relief to hang out with Peter more because there's some way that it feels less loaded emotionally than with a woman friend. We can be playmates without any heavy stuff, and that's enough for him. [*With an ironic shrug*] The problem is that it's not always enough for me; I get hungry for all those emotional complications with my women friends.

The boundaries that keep a man separate from others—and against which a woman might rail when in a love relationship with him—in a friendship, afford a respite from the emotional intensity that's almost always present in a close relationship with a woman. Trying to explain the difference, a forty-seven-year-old executive secretary said:

> There's a hard edge you come up against in dealing with a man that I appreciate sometimes. I don't quite know how to say it, but there's a kind of safety in it. It doesn't let you forget who you are. [*Sitting quietly for a moment*] That's not all, though. It's not that I think men are smarter than women, but their intellectual style is so different that it's easier to deal with sometimes. In some ways I can take criticism and give it more easily with a man friend. We women are always worried about a relationship or hurting someone's feelings—things like that—so things can sometimes get irritatingly mushy and messy.

This "mushiness" of which she spoke came up time and again, and always ambivalently, as women compared their friendships with men and with women. At one level, the women who talked about it found it troubling, some saying that, because women tend to be so concerned about another's feelings, it was difficult to fully trust either a compliment or a criticism.

"How can I believe she means I look good when she says it automatically, every time I see her?"

"Mostly when women criticize each other, it gets so hedged around and softened up that you can't be sure what it really means."

At another level, however, there is a deep appreciation of the care and sensitivity with which a woman friend is likely to avoid giving pain or offense in a moment of vulnerability. So the same woman who talked about being able to "take criticism and give it more easily with a man friend" also said:

> I complain about things getting messy between women, but I don't forget the thousand times I've been grateful because a friend cared enough not to tell me the truth.

Both men and women, then, find that their differences bind them while they also separate them. The "hard edge" men present makes it easier for a woman to deal more directly with a male friend, while it also frustrates her. The concern that women display for process that can be so irritating to a man also underlies the nurturance for which he turns to her so eagerly. They each maintain a love-hate ambivalence toward the other's different intellectual and emotional styles, both getting something they want or need from the other's mode, while also feeling it alien and oppressive at times. A man's ability to separate his emotional and cognitive sides, to have women friends for one and men for the other, saves him from the kind of frustration women feel in these friendships. But because a woman is less able than a man to sunder these parts of herself, she tends to be less comfortable with the kind of accommodation he seems to make so easily, more broadly critical of the quality of her friendships with men.

Despite their criticisms of men as friends, however, some women still look to men for a definition of self. So, for example, a twenty-seven-year-old public health nurse who said, "I can go away for a week with a man and in three days be yearning to come home and talk from the heart to my friend Judy," was equally clear that no woman, no matter how valued or close, could affirm her self-esteem, her sense of worth as person-in-the-world, as a man could.

> I love being with a man because men have such good ideas about things. I always get very stimulated, like they just open up different worlds for me.

"A few minutes ago you said you can hardly wait to get home to Judy when you've gone away with a man. How does that fit with what you said just now?" I asked.

> Men are more stimulating, that's all. I love Judy and I need her to talk to from my heart. But I learn things from men, and my men

> friends have had a lot more influence on me in terms of developing interests and things like that. Their ideas are more important than women's ideas because they think about things women don't think about. So if I get praise from a man, it means a lot; I mean, it *really* counts.

"Does it mean more to you than the same praise from a woman?"

> [*Looking down at her hands to cover her discomfort*] Yeah. I know it's not supposed to be that way anymore, but it would mean more, a lot more. If Judy tells me I'm smart or wonderful or whatever, it's one thing. But if my friend Jack tells it to me, it means a lot more.

"Could you say what it is that makes you feel that way?" I asked.

> I'm not real sure. It's like they're right—men, I mean. If they make a statement, I tend to believe them more than a woman and to put more weight on it because [*her words trailing*] . . . I don't really know why. Their words always seem more important to me, that's all. So naturally getting praise from a man makes me feel wonderful, like I really count too.

There's nothing "natural" about feeling more "wonderful" in getting praise from a man than from a woman, however. It's simply a confirmation of the greater status and prestige men have in the world, therefore of the power they still have to define a woman, to validate her identity, to affirm her sense of self and her worth.

Few women spoke so openly about this aspect of their friendships with men. Undoubtedly, this is due largely to the years of feminist struggle which have helped women to value themselves and their friendships with each other anew. Many women, therefore, no longer look only to men for evidence of their worth.

But despite the fact that the current ideological climate

makes such open admissions embarrassing, I also found undeniable evidence that, for considerable numbers of women, a man's estimate is still what they value most highly. Especially among women who are less educated, therefore confined to low-level, dead-end jobs thought to be unfit for a man—work that largely fulfills women's traditional function of service to men—the authority of a man's word, the status to be derived from a connection with a man, the vicarious identity to be achieved through him, all remain influential in defining self and affirming worth.

It's not just among women who work in traditional jobs and live relatively traditional lives that this is the case, however. Among highly educated and successful professional women as well, a man's attention and admiration for something beyond her abilities in the traditional woman's spheres can still count more highly than a woman's. "I'm not proud of it, but I think it feels different to have a male friend who admires my intellect because it's like telling the world I'm smart enough," said a university professor reluctantly.

Partly she credits such male attention so highly because, for most of her life, men have worn the mantle of expertise; partly because it's so much harder for a woman to command that kind of attention from a man in the male world of power and authority; partly because there are so few women there to give it to her. Even now, when women are beginning to challenge men in the professional world, pleasing and impressing a man is still the requirement for entering it and making one's way in it. For men remain the gatekeepers—deciding not just who gets in and who stays out, but who stands still and who climbs up the ladder as well. A very successful thirty-five-year-old attorney spoke vehemently about these issues:

> I live very largely in a man's world at work. All the other partners in my firm are men; I'm the only woman. The courts are run by men, for men; the opposing attorney is most likely going to be a

man. In that kind of setting, it's hard to get away from it. When I go up against a man in court and win, I have to admit, I feel different than when I beat a woman. I'm almost ashamed to say it, but it's like he's *really* a worthy adversary. And when he says, "Good show, Joan," or something like that, I *know* I've been complimented.

"How do you account for those feelings?" I wanted to know. "Why is a man a 'worthy adversary' in a way a woman is not?"

Christ, that's hard to answer, isn't it? [*With a sharp release of her breath*] Maybe it's because they still own the world and define what's good and bad. Now that I think about it, how can it be otherwise? From the time I was a little kid, I knew I could get my mother's approval, but I had to work hard for my father's. He was too busy to notice me unless I was being outstanding. Now every step I take up the ladder depends on a man's evaluation of me, not a woman's. It's a setup! Even though women are vastly more important to me in some ways—and honestly, I do respect women—there's still a cachet about what a man thinks of me that I can't deny.

It's a vicious circle for women, as it is for any devalued group in a society: They internalize the social definition of self as inferior, then turn to those who formulated that definition, and who now have a stake in maintaining it, for reassurance that it isn't true. In doing so, they help to increase the power of the powerful.

There is no greater power, nor a more heinous abuse of it, than the ability of those who are powerful in a society to define selfhood for those who are not. This is why the powerful so jealously guard this particular aspect of their dominion—why, for example, the "Black is beautiful" movement of the early civil rights days created such antagonism among whites. In rejecting the dominant society's standards of beauty and desirability, which historically have ruled blacks out of the competition, they threatened to strip white racism of one important aspect of its power. For the same reasons, feminism has been seen as an ominous presence in the modern world. As women have begun to take unto themselves the right to define self in all its capacities, men have reacted in fear and anxiety to the erosion of this historic and heretofore unquestioned power.

Given the traditional inequity in power between men and women, then, it's no surprise that a woman will still look to a man for affirmation of those parts of herself that have for so long been denied. It's this imbalance also that makes it possible for a man to expose his vulnerabilities to a woman in the same way the wealthy traditionally have exposed themselves to their servants. Both woman and servant don't count.

It's less threatening, too, with a woman who's clearly a friend than with a lover—or a woman he hopes to make into one. Once romance enters, the power relations shift. She becomes someone he must reckon with, at least until she's caught and secured in the bonds of marriage. But outside a romantic love relationship, a woman is not a threat of any consequence, not someone whose estimate of him matters in the world, not a serious competitor for status, prestige, honor—for any of the rewards men prize so highly. It's another man who really counts, another man for whom he must put on the show of strength and invulnerability, another man against whom his sense of self and his efficacy in the world are tested and defined. She is, after all, "only a woman."

It makes little difference, either, how high her status is—whether she is in a more powerful position in the world than the man—the same dynamic is at work between them, as I have noticed repeatedly in my clinical work.[11] Most of the men I have seen over the years had already spent some considerable time with male therapists, most of them competent professionals. Yet when they came into my office, there was little to show for the work they had done. With a woman, however, they soon found themselves able to move deeply inside themselves, to expose fantasies and vulnerabilities that, they said, they never dared touch before. Why? The answer, I believe, lies, at least in part, in the characteristic interactions between men and women I have been discussing here, in the fact that it is a man who is the worthy competitor, not a woman.

The blank screen with which a psychotherapist is expected to come to the clinical interaction is a fantasy, and a male one at that. Even if, as human beings, we could really put ourselves "in neutral," we still come to the clinical setting as man or as woman—gendered selves with profound implications for what will go on between therapist and patient. It isn't just the patient's projections that come into play, nor is it his or her expectations alone. Rather both patient and therapist bring to the clinical setting a lifetime of social and psychological experience in a gendered world, their distinctive male and female styles, and their characteristic ways of interacting with same-sex and opposite-sex others.

I don't mean that a male psychotherapist is less skilled than a woman or less capable of the warmth and empathy necessary to a satisfactory therapeutic outcome. But there's not much reason to believe that the kind of classic competitive interaction between men that we know so well would suddenly disappear. Rather it's quite likely that, even in the therapeutic setting, the powerful one finds himself defending his primacy and the other attacking it, an interaction that bodes ill for the kind of self-exposure psychotherapy requires. With a woman as therapist and the same man as patient, however, his guard is down, his competitive strivings muted, if not entirely gone. She is, after all, "only a woman."

I am not unaware of transference issues between them, of the many levels that are stimulated by the therapeutic relationship, of the way her presence and authority also evoke within him the fears and fantasies of early childhood when mother seemed so powerful. But just as he needed to devalue her then as a way of containing his fears and easing the separation, so he can invoke the same defensive maneuver in therapy with a woman.

It's not in consciousness that all this goes on, of course. That's precisely the problem. For once the internal dynamics of our interactions move from the unconscious to the conscious, we have the power to change them. But to offer them up for interpretation and examination so that we could accomplish such change, both psychological theory and its practitioners would have to become more conscious of the impact of the social and psychological experience of gender on the clinical setting.

There is, however, one set of relationships between women and men that is not so troubled by all the issues I have recounted here—the friendships between gay men and women, lesbian or heterosexual. No one knows how widespread these friendships are, but in their book entitled *Homosexualities,* sociologists Alan Bell and Martin Weinberg report that about two-thirds of the homosexual men they studied have friendships with women.[12] Among the gay men I met, well over half said they had at least one close female friend, most often a straight woman.[13]

Interestingly, only about one-fifth of the lesbians I interviewed claimed a male friend, and among these women, it was far more often a gay man than a straight one. The lesbian/gay male friendships need little interpretation or explanation, since it seems reasonable that lesbians would be more comfortable with men who share their homosexual orientation and who, therefore, are defined as the oppressed rather than as the oppressor. But the fact that these friendships seem to be far less common than those between straight women and gay men is worth a comment. Speculating about the reasons, John Malone, author of *Straight Women/Gay Men,* writes that "lesbians apparently feel they have more in common with straight women than with either gay or straight men"[14]—a speculation confirmed by my own research which shows that lesbians do not feel nearly as isolated from other women as gay men do from their straight brothers. Therefore, friendships with men, gay or straight, are not a compelling priority for lesbians.[15]

More interesting, however, is the paucity of lesbian/straight men friendships, which, I believe, is related to the historic antagonisms between men and women. The lesbian, radicalized by the women's and the gay rights movements, is likely to be angry enough at heterosexual men for their oppression of both women and gays so that a friendship with such a man is of small interest. On his part, the straight man, whose sense of his manhood is importantly related to seeing a sexually desirable reflection of himself in the eyes of a woman, more often than not sees a woman who has renounced heterosexuality as something of a threat, therefore also as either an affront or a freak.

But friendships between straight women and gay men are relatively common in any situation where these two come to know each other, whether among the more highly educated or the less so. Thus women who live in any community or work in any industry where gay men have made a prominent place for themselves—the worlds of beauty, fashion, interior design, theater or publishing, for instance—often have strong friendships with homosexual men that they describe in terms very different from those women use about their straight male friends. A forty-one-year-old beautician, married for twenty-four years, said of her work and the friendships she has formed there:

> One of the things I like about where I work is the people. I worked in an office once and I hated it because the men were always so snooty and bossy to the girls there, always ordering them around and expecting us to jump when they called. But here, we're more equal, the men and women. Of course, they're all gay, and that makes a big difference. I couldn't be real friends with a straight man, but a gay man's different.

"How so?" I asked.

> It's lots more like having a woman friend. I can talk to my friend Denny like I can to Carol, even though he's still a man. [*Biting her lip as she stopped to think*] It's funny, because I know he's still a man, but there's something different about him. He treats me different too—like I'm more of an equal.
>
> He's interested in lots of the same things I am. I mean, when

> he tells a story, it's like listening to a girl friend. With most of the men I know, even my husband, it's just like, "Here's the facts; don't bother me with anything else." But gay men are different; they talk about things more like women do, and they like to talk about a lot of the same things too—like clothes, and people, and things like that.

The issue of equality is something straight women stressed about their relationships with gay men, and the notion that gay men "talk about things more like women do" is widespread. A few women spoke also of how the friendship helps them to understand a male view of the world without raising the doubts, anxieties and pretensions that beset a relationship with a straight man.

This is one place where men's and women's perceptions of the friendship, of what it means to them, did not differ widely. Generally the men talked of appreciating a woman's company, of valuing the feminine perspective, of feeling confirmed and respected in their friendships with straight women in ways they too often did not when dealing with heterosexual men. Explaining why such a friendship is important to his sense of himself and his ongoing struggle to feel positively about his homosexuality, a successful thirty-seven-year-old graphic artist said:

> I still live two lives, and many of my clients don't know I'm gay. It's not that I hide it exactly; I just don't advertise. Most of my income comes from the large corporate world, and that's not a place where you'd want to spread it around. So my friends are either other men who are gay or they're women, because that's who I have most in common with and can be myself with.

"Are you saying you have more in common with a straight woman than a straight man?" I asked.

> Not universally, but mostly that's absolutely right. [*Looking off into space for a moment or two*] How can I say it? I find women have an aesthetic sensibility that's closer to my own. So I can go to a concert or a museum or the theater with a woman friend, and

it feels wonderfully compatible in a way I can't imagine it being with the straight men I know. Or if I'm having trouble in my love life, I can talk to a woman about it easily. Can you just see me telling some straight guy about that, with all that homophobia they have?

For gay men and straight women, then, the alliance seems a natural one, their friendships bringing a kind of comfort and companionship that neither can find easily in the world of heterosexual men where both have been devalued so consistently and for so long. For women who, in recent years, have found themselves struggling toward a greater internal sense of equality and independence, and for homosexual men who are in the process of internalizing a more positive sense of their homosexuality, the sympathetic understanding and moral support they can offer each other are precious aids to the emergence of a new and valued sense of self.

I don't mean to suggest that these friendships are without strain. When they are single, both gay men and straight women complain, as so many single people of any sexual orientation do, that they feel neglected and abandoned when a new romance enters the life of a friend. When they are married or mated, the complications also may be no different than among straight marrieds and their individual friends—the mate who's jealous about the connection between the friends, about the intimacy they share; the single friend who feels she or he must always take second place to the needs and demands of a mate. Nevertheless, these are the friendships across the gender line that seem to afford the greatest equality and the fewest tensions.[16]

Except for these relationships between women and gay men, then, our cross-sex friendships are marked by contradiction and ambivalence, as are so many of our relations with each other. We each get something we need from the other, something we cannot easily get in same-sex friendships; and at the same time, we miss something as well. We each look to the other to fill the missing half; and we each find some gratifications, some frustrations.

For both, an opposite-sex friendship calls upon a part of self that's usually less readily accessible when relating to same-sex friends. For a man, a woman friend allows him to reach his more emotional side, to experience his vulnerability, to treat himself and his friend more tenderly than is permissible with male friends. But he misses the kind of rough camaraderie he can have with another man. For a woman, friendship with a man helps her to reach her tougher side, the harder edge that's kept under wraps in relationships with women. A man friend, too, can help her to maintain her separateness, to affirm her place in the world outside the relationship sphere. But she misses the intensity of the emotional connection she can have with a woman.

Thus, while highly valued, friendships that cross the gender line usually remain what I would call "special purpose" friendships—relationships that, for whatever reasons, have a set of built-in limitations. For men, the limitations are relatively unobjectionable, different from those they find in their relations with other men but still part of the limits they generally expect and experience in any friendship. But women are more likely to look for more "general purpose" relationships—those that have the potential to tap the many layers and parts of self, that offer the intimacy they seek. Thus they are inclined to chafe at the limitations in friendships with men and to look toward relationships with women for the depth and intensity they need and want.

9

Best Friends

Best friends: a special kind of relationship, and a unique one, embodying the best of all the important relationships in our lives—kin, mate and friend—along with the problems of all three, and some that belong to friendship alone. These are the friends who come closest to our fantasies about friendship. And these also are the friends who can bring us both our greatest joys and our sorriest disappointments.

As with mates or lovers, best friends raise for each other most sharply many of the needs and desires stimulated by the original infantile relationship with mother while also being part of those neglected relationships we call "friendship." Whether explicit or not, there's a promise in a best friendship—a promise of mutual love, concern, protection, understanding and, not least of all, stability and durability that separates this relationship from others we call "friend." There's a particular urgency between best friends, therefore, that seems to seek constant reassurance—a tension that has no easy resolution, that brings to the friendship a poignancy that's born perhaps of the experience of all the friends who have passed through our lives and are long gone.

In childhood and adolescence, best friendships usually come and go rapidly, although not easily and not without pain, as the testimony of many of the people I interviewed made clear. Years, even decades later, women and men still spoke with emotion about the failure of an adolescent best friendship, wondering what happened to the friend, fantasizing about what it would be like to meet again, recalling the pain of the rupture, the sense of betrayal, the terrible loneliness that followed.

In adulthood, best friendships are usually more stable than those of earlier periods, and also more variable. When an older child or adolescent calls someone a best friend, the relationship may be short-lived, but while it exists, it's almost certain that there's a deep emotional connection between the friends, that they see each other often, relate intensely, share intimately. When an adult says, "This is my best friend," however, that's the beginning of knowledge about the relationship, not the end. For, as with all friendships, the words "best friend" cover such a wide range of relationships that, in themselves, they cannot tell us much about any individual friendship.

Not everyone has a best friend or wants one.[1] People make best friends and lose them for the same variety of reasons that all friendships are made and broken—time, distance, unresolved conflicts, changes in one or both friends that make the friendship untenable. I met people who hadn't seen or spoken with a best friend in weeks, even months, and others who were in touch several times a week. Some of the best friendships I encountered were relatively recent, untested yet by time and circumstance; others were long-lived, having survived ten, twenty, even thirty years. Given the geographic mobility of American society, I was not surprised to find people who were separated from a best friend by large distances—a situation I found particularly interesting and provocative.

Sometimes, as I have said also of other friendships, these long-distance relationships exist in memory only, the distance having robbed them of their *raison d'être.* Yet even such "best friends" serve a function for those who must hold on to the fantasy. To the extent that people continue to believe in these mythic relationships, they form a defense against experiencing the reality of the loneliness that must be theirs.[2]

Often enough, however, this was not the case. Many people maintain long-distance friendships, even best friendships, that are vital and alive—relationships that are kept that way through regular contact by phone, letter and intermittent visits. Such relationships are more likely to be found among professional middle-class people who have studied in one part of the country and now work in another, women and men who travel easily and relatively often for both professional and personal reasons to the places they left behind.

Frequently, of course, people maintain an important emotional link with best friends of the past while also developing new intimate relationships where they live. Sometimes, however, friendships from afar serve a need for attachment and a level of intimacy that a person finds more difficult to sustain with someone who lives nearby. The distance itself ensures a certain emotional safety, allowing for much more control than is possible with a friend who is close at hand.

Contact that takes place largely by telephone and letter allows for a peculiar kind of intimacy in that we can speak or write about deeply felt matters while we are also protected from the unexpected or unplanned messages conveyed in a face-to-face encounter. If I am speaking directly to a friend, I watch for the signs of her reaction to my words, just as she watches my facial expressions and body postures to fill out the message my words withhold. But the telephone protects both of us. The signs of her approval or disapproval, restlessness or boredom, and so on, are not visible to me; the symptoms that would signal the depth of my distress not accessible to her. Letters, of course, provide even less possibility than the telephone for an immediate or unintended response, therefore more control and more protection for both participants.

Such long-distance best friendships share some of the qualities of the therapist-patient relationship. Both permit intimacy while, at the same time, preserving distance; both allow discretion in what is revealed, how much and when; both promise safety from well-meaning but unwanted intrusions.

We can confide a personal problem to a therapist or to a long-distance friend with some certainty that intimacies revealed are safe from the immediate circle of friends and family, without fear that we'll run into the confidante in the supermarket and have to face the question, spoken or unspoken, "Is everything okay?" We can share something of our fears and fantasies with some assurance that we will not confront a reaction that's difficult or painful. The responses of both will be safely hidden from view—the therapist's because of training, the friend's because of distance.

But most best friends live close by. And all the differences between them notwithstanding, these relationships generally share certain common characteristics. Usually the label "best friend" signifies a level of attachment, of intimacy, of commitment, of sharing, that transcends all other friendships—a relationship not bounded by the usual limits that constrain friends. As one woman, a fifty-two-year-old housewife, said:

> One of the ways I think of friendship is that each relationship has limits, even the most intimate ones. For me, it's been useful to think about my friendships in terms of where the final limit is visible and acknowledged. Then two people accommodate to that limit and try to work within it.
>
> But there's always one or two relationships where you can push at those limits, just like you can in a good marriage. That's the really intimate friendship. With Marsha, my closest friend, we've pushed them very far and there's no sign of having reached them yet. We're even willing to be bored by each other sometimes. When you can be together and even feel bored, that's something to value enormously because most relationships don't survive those kinds of feelings.

As with both kin and mate, the relationship between best friends must survive all kinds of feelings—the "good" ones and the "bad" ones, the loving ones and the hateful ones, the ones that make us reach for intense intimacy one moment and for cool distance the next, even the ones that signal boredom with each other.

More than others, best friends are drawn together in much the same way as lovers—by something ineffable, something to which, most people say, it is almost impossible to give words. Whether speaking of the initial meeting or of the process by which the friendship was established, people often talk as if something happened to them in the same way they "happened" to fall in love and marry.

"When I met her, I just knew. It's like when I met my husband I said, 'That's the man I'm going to marry.' I looked at her that time we met and I knew."

"It just happened, what can I say?"

"When I met Pete I had the kind of experience I've had with women rather than with a man—I mean, women I've fallen in love with. There was this sense of fit, suddenly, overwhelmingly and instantly."

"It's funny, I don't know how to say it. There was something there . . . ," hesitating as she searched for the words. Unable to find them, she began anew, "Well, it started out being . . . ," another pause as she found herself at a loss again. Finally giving up the attempt, "It's like fate."

Not all best friendships start with a bang, of course. Sometimes they simply grow without thought or consciousness. People meet, come to know and respect each other, grow a little closer with each shared experience, with the passage of time, eventually come to call themselves best friends. "It's not something I thought about. He was just a nice guy; we liked doing the same things; we got along great; and he sort of became my best friend."

Whatever the actual experience, whatever the chronology of events, as with a lover or a mate, most friends come together out of some combination of attraction to the other and their internal psychological needs and desires. In a romance, the sexual figures prominently and consciously in the relationship, from initial attraction to its consummation. In a friendship, the explicitly sexual is muted, if not fully out of consciousness, in favor of a more diffuse attraction to the total personality, although most people are at least somewhat aware of the appeal of the physical.

"There was something about the way she looked that attracted me."

"The whole way she was put together engaged me from the start."

"My initial attraction to anyone, whether it's a love affair with a woman or a friendship with a man, is to a person who has a kind of tall, cool, blond, or at least fair good looks that, for me, is like bait to a fish."

In both love and friendship, if a relationship is to grow beyond the initial attraction, there must also be some sharing of values, of an aesthetic sensibility, of intellect, of interest and, perhaps most important of all, some way in which the friend or lover reaches a part of self not accessible to most others. A forty-two-year-old psychiatrist, specializing in family therapy, explained his relationship with his best friend this way:

> My best friend is Dan. I've been aware for a long time that he's exactly the same temperamentally as the women I fall in love with. My ex-wife, the woman I'm with now, and Dan all have brought a certain kind of irrationality and emotional instability and need to the relationship. I bring the other side—more solid, reasonable, reassuring, rational.
>
> I can be close to other kinds of people, but for someone to touch me as deeply as those three have, these qualities are essential. I can feel safe and comforted by meeting their needs for reason and stability and, at the same time, they allow me to feel more deeply than I can without someone like that in my life. Maybe it's a little crazy, but the fit is good, like a hand in a glove, so mostly it works.

We enter into such relationships out of a complex interaction between our own needs and those of the other. We feel safe in them, safe in the knowledge that we can give the other something she or he needs, something that will create a binding tie between us. Somewhere inside, we may also know the friend or lover we have chosen has qualities we need, qualities we envy because we cannot yet give them to ourselves.

The whole issue of envy—so important and so maligned a part of our relations with each other—deserves some special comment here. In the traditional psychoanalytic view, espoused most forcefully perhaps by Melanie Klein, envy is seen as resting on a greedy wish to take something from another.[3] Envy, therefore, becomes a threat to any relationship, something that must be contained and controlled, a cause for shame.

Yet many of us can recall feelings of envy that are not accompanied by a wish to destroy. A friend has a social life that's richer and fuller than ours, a colleague accomplishes something we wish we had done, a sibling has some material goods or comforts we miss—all these can be cause for envy. But whether the feelings become a force for destruction or a part of a creative effort at mastery is not foretold by their existence alone. For envy, as with other suspect emotional states—anger, for example—can be felt in varying degrees of intensity and with positive effects, as well as negative ones, on both the person who experiences it and the relationship within which it is experienced.

About the negative potential of envy and its corrosive effects, much has been written. But what has not yet been understood, it seems to me, is that envy, and the way we use it, is related to the level of self-development—to whether we carry inside us a satisfying sense of self, one that feels rich and full, or whether our inner experience is of a self that's empty and impoverished.

For the person who experiences an inner void, envy will take shape as it has been classically described—a greedy impulse to wrest the desired object from the other in an attempt to ease the pain, to fill up the vacant space inside, to shore up the infantile and needy self. But for the one with a relatively well developed, satisfying sense of self, envy can become a creative internal force. Then, rather than the destructive wish to deprive another, envy can be a goad to greater self-fulfillment—a reminder of tasks yet undone, of possibilities untapped. Then, the wish to have a similar valued quality can impel us into using the relationship within which envy is brought to the fore to learn about and master the felt deficit, goading us into greater self-fulfillment.

Such personal change as may come out of this use of envy may, in some circumstances, be good for the individual and bad for the relationship, whether a best friendship or a marriage. We may be unconsciously drawn to another because we find in him or her the missing parts of self. The woman who fears her emotional intensity and the man who is worried about his inability to feel deeply enough, as described by the man above, are a good example and a common one: She feels the need for the restraint he supplies, and he for the excitement she brings to his life.

Some people may be content forever to let the other fill those missing parts. But often enough, with time and experience, one partner in a relationship develops a sufficiently strong sense of self to envy the other those qualities, to want to make them her or his own, to believe it can be done. When that happens, the woman may come to understand that she needs no external controls to feel safe, or the man that he needs no excitement from outside to feel alive. Then the perfect fit, "like a hand in a glove," no longer works so well.

This unprecedented lack of fit can be fatal to a relationship. With the complementary matching of missing parts gone, the symbiotic attachment that bound them together will shift as well, leaving one or both partners anxious and fearful, set adrift—as if the rudder that had, until then, set the course of the relationship was suddenly broken.

But where creative struggle is possible between two people—a struggle that might well have its origins in the envy of one of them—the discovery of the mismatch and the feelings it stirs can become a spur to personal growth. Then each partner can use the safety of the intimate environment, and the model of an alternative way of being that the friend or mate provides, to develop in self the part that was missing. As each moves in the direction of a firmer sense of a separate and autonomous self, the stage is set for a freer, more differentiated and more mature relationship.

Which way it will go depends on the individuals involved, on their capacity to use an intimate relationship to learn about self and other, on their ability to tolerate ambiguity as they search for a new balance, test out new ways of being, discover unknown strengths. Not an easy task, to be sure, but within the reach of each of us so long as we can conceive of such shifts and changes in a relationship as challenges and opportunities rather than as setbacks and betrayals.

Best friends have the power to help and to hurt in ways that no one but a mate or a lover can match. The intensity of the emotional relationship, for example, can lead to the kinds of jealousies and rivalries that recall the scenes of childhood between siblings, as this from a forty-three-year-old woman, the branch manager in a large savings and loan organization, tells us:

> I love Bonnie as much as I've ever cared about anyone in this world, but I've never had a relationship, even with my husband, that's so complicated. I don't think of myself as a terribly competitive person, but with her I can get into what feels like an all-out war inside me. She can make me angrier than just about anyone too, except Dick, of course. I've tried to figure it out because it makes me feel bad, and the best I can get is that it's a lot like I felt with my sister when we were kids. Only I love Bonnie, I really do; I don't think I ever loved my sister, not then and not now.

The old rivalry with the sister is there, to be sure, but this time in a relationship where she can also feel the love she missed then, still misses now. It's just this quality of emotional depth that permits best friends the opportunity to redo the past in ways that enable the healing of the old pain.

Another woman, a thirty-three-year-old high-school teacher, speaking of her older sister and the difficulties in that relationship, told of the way her best friend, a few years older than she, has become the good sister she wanted so badly—one who lends her clothes, who introduces her to her friends, who lets her share her "toys."

> One of the things I get from Elaine is the kind of love and approval I never got from my older sister. There was always too much jealousy between us, I guess, and all that little kid–big kid stuff that's probably natural with siblings. I wanted to tag after her, but she didn't want me around. Or maybe I'd start to play with something of hers, and she'd see me and take it away and give me a wallop. I was always dying to wear her clothes when I got a little older, just to feel like a big girl, but she'd never let me. With Elaine, she'd give me the shirt off her back. [*With a reflective smile*] In fact, she has.

Although the reworking of the troubled sibling relationship is part of the glue in this best friendship, it is, of course, not all that holds it together and that makes it so important to the women who share it. Both also talked about the respect and admiration they feel for each other, about the shared intellectual, emotional and social life that binds them. Both told also about how they have stood by each other "through thick and thin"—through conflicts in the marriage of one of them, through illness in the family of the other, through periods when they felt angry and disenchanted with each other.

Unlike other friendships, where expectations are more modest, we usually expect our best friends to meet us at many different levels. We want best friends to respond to the many selves inside us, to understand our feelings and, if not to share them, at least to know their value. A thirty-eight-year-old artist, married fourteen years, said of her best friend:

> The fundamental thing about my friendship with Nancy, and what I prize so, is that I feel free to be all the different things I am with her—including a depressed drag sometimes. I don't have to be on stage or be clever and amusing for her to want to be with me. It's like there's a sign on our friendship for both of us that says, "No cute persona wanted here; only the real stuff."
>
> She's not an artist but she has such a deep appreciation of my artistic side that it thrills me. Except for Stuart, she's the only person in years who I've felt understands me in my core self.

"No cute persona wanted here; only the real stuff." To be known and understood, to be valued for the complexity and variety that is our self—these are the expectations among best friends, the same as with a mate. Yet for most of us, as I have said, there are differences, both in expectations and in the limits of permissible behaviors. In response to my question about these differences, the same woman explained:

> It's hard to say whether the limits or what I expect are so different or whether they're just of a different order. My life isn't tied to Nancy's in the same way as it is with Stuart where what happens to one of us profoundly affects the other. In general, I guess I'd say that the family pulls and tugs at you in a more primary way. So yes, I suppose I'd have to grant that the expectations are different on all sides.

It's true, of course, that we expect less from friends, no matter how close, than we do from those with whom our lives are bound in one way or another. It's also true that friends tend to respect boundaries and permit distance in ways that are much more difficult for lovers or mates. Comparing the difference between her best friend and her lover, a twenty-seven-year-old office worker complained:

> It's hard to tell Ed I don't want to see him because I'm in a bad mood, or maybe just because I need to be alone for a bit. He'll get pouty and feel rejected. Or if he doesn't do that, he'll try to convince me I'll feel better if he's here, and . . . Oh, hell, it's sometimes easier just to let it be his way. Now with Trish, I can say the same thing and right away she understands. I don't get pressured, and I don't have to feel guilty.

This is one of the gifts a best friend offers, one of the qualities for which we value a best friend most—the intense intimacy we share which, at the same time, respects our boundaries in ways that relations with a lover or a mate generally do not. But since there is no institutional form to honor the best friend relationship, and even fewer rules than with a lover to define the role, we're likely to tolerate far less emotional distress and conflict with a friend before calling it quits.

This, indeed, is one of the bitterest complaints I heard about friends and friendship—person after person telling tales about intimate friendships that failed. Most people try to make sense of the experience, so in the same way they try to comprehend what motivates a divorce, they find reasons—reasons that never seem wholly satisfactory to them, especially if they are the person who was left.

"In the furthest reaches of my imagination, I never dreamed my friendship with Ellen would come to an end. Yet it did, and I'll never fully understand why," said a woman as she struggled to hold back tears.

"We just changed, that's all," Ellen said tartly when we met. "She couldn't accept that. She kept wanting me to be just like her, and I wasn't anymore. Maybe I never was, I don't know."

When a best friendship preexists a marriage, there's likely to be serious trouble as allegiances begin to shift, and the balance between the friends' needs for intimacy and distance with each other begins to change, as the story of this failed friendship shows. Speaking with difficulty, so freshly did she still feel the hurt, a forty-four-year-old woman, a nutritionist, said:

I guess what happened is really complicated, but in the last year of the friendship, I was getting angry at Janet all the time. It all started after she got involved with the man she's going to marry. I felt as if she was withdrawing from me. I'd get angry and tell her, but I didn't get any satisfaction. I think if she could have admitted it, I wouldn't have had to push so hard. But she didn't. The upshot was that she felt I wanted too much from her and she ended up saying she didn't want that kind of close relationship with me anymore.

As she told her side of the story, Janet, a thirty-seven-year-old legal secretary, could hardly contain her anger.

I had this very, very close relationship with this woman Marlene. We used to rely on each other as people do in a sexual relationship often, although we weren't sexual. I mean, we saw each other several times a week; we would take care of each other when we were sick, things like that. But she felt pushed aside when I got involved with Jerry. She wasn't willing to make certain compromises for me being in a family, and it became impossible to continue a relationship with her.

Both women agree that something changed between them when a man came into the life of one of them. But it wasn't just a new love that threatened the friendship. Rather the larger problem lies in the fact that, although profoundly important in our lives, the position of the best friend remains an anomaly.

Because of the emotional intensity of a best friendship, it touches some of our most primitive internal needs and responses in much the same way as do our love relationships—normally less acutely, perhaps, but still difficult to contain. A best friendship, therefore, stimulates the wish for exclusivity. Even the name we give it—*best* friend—facilitates the fantasy that the wish can become reality, or at the very least, that first place will be forever ours. When the illusion is threatened, people talk about being "betrayed," "abandoned," even about being "jilted." As one fifty-year-old statistician, married twenty-five years, put it:

> Maybe it's crazy, but when my best friend began to pull away a little, I felt more like a jilted lover than a friend who'd been knocked down a notch or two in importance. It wasn't good enough to be just one of her close friends, not after what we shared for so many years.

Given the feelings these relationships evoke, it's no surprise that they often become a source of conflict with a mate, stimulating jealousy in ways that other friendships may not. For the intensity of the attachment, the breadth of shared values and interests, and the aura of romance surrounding a best friendship, especially at its beginnings, threaten the exclusive commitment that marriage partners usually insist upon. The thirty-year-old wife of a man who shares an intense bond with his best friend said:

> I don't mind his going out with the boys once in awhile, but I sometimes think this friendship he has with Mike is a little kinky or something. They're together all the time, and it's like my life has to revolve around Mike, not his life around me. It doesn't seem right.

And a forty-six-year-old husband, speaking of his wife and her best friend, admitted:

> She thinks I don't like her friend Peg, but that's not it. [*Uncomfortably*] I guess maybe I'm jealous. When they first met, I swear, you'd think they were having some kind of a love affair the way they were always trying to figure out ways to get together and talking on the phone all the time. Why would I feel good about that? You can be damn sure she'd hate it if I had someone else that important in my life.

Indeed, there's something to be said for their concern. I don't mean it's apt, only that it's not wholly irrational given our belief in the "happily ever after" fantasy, given our expectation that a mate will complete us, will meet all our needs, will be exclusively ours. It is such expectations that are irrational, as is the society that continues to promulgate them even in the face of a divorce rate that is so staggeringly high.

Yet just as there are marriages that survive their complex emotional entanglements, so there are best friendships that do too. A forty-nine-year-old woman, herself a clinical psychologist who had several years of her own personal therapy behind her, was able to articulate quite clearly something of the process of her relationship with her best friend, what motivated it at the start, and how it has survived the shifts and changes that came their way:

> For many years, my closest friend, Marianna, was the good mother I needed very badly. My own mother is a woman who will tell you with pride that she has no women friends and that she doesn't trust a woman doctor because they're not smart enough or good enough.
>
> I know now that, along with devaluing other women—which, of course, means me too—this means she doesn't value herself either. But I didn't know that then. I only knew I was very taken with Marianna when we met and that we seemed to have a lot in common. I was pleased and flattered that she liked me and took me seriously because I didn't really expect that from a woman. So in the early stages, my relationship with Marianna was really an exploration about how you can be in a relationship with another woman and be safe and trusting and self-respecting.

"That was the beginning of your relationship," I observed. "Is that still what keeps you tied, or have things changed between you?" With a broad smile, she replied:

> No, no, that was then. I think I've finally outgrown that mother-daughter stuff. Now we come together like two adults who have a shared history, and a very long one, and who are also interested in many of the same things at the same time. There's a large common well of interest and experience between us.

"Does the change make the friendship less charged or perhaps even less important for you?" I asked.

> Less charged, yes. I don't need that kind of support for my self-esteem and for my actual sense of myself as a woman and a professional person that I needed then. So I don't have to be so greedy about the friendship as I used to be. Also, we have such a long history by now that I don't worry anymore about the relationship and its existence. I just know we'll always be there for each other in one way or another.
>
> But you also asked whether the friendship is less important. That's harder to answer. Let's see. We've both grown and changed over the fifteen years we've known each other, and we need different things from each other now. So in many ways the friendship is less intense than it used to be. Also I think we both have other sources of support that we didn't have before. When I say those things, it sounds as if I'm saying it *is* less important now. But I don't think that's really true. It's still very important and still one of the central relationships in my life, but in quite a different way.
>
> As I think about it, maybe it's the wrong question. In a friendship of such long standing, I imagine there are always times of more or less closeness and need and importance. It's like a marriage that goes through different phases and is very close for periods of time, then not so close at other times.

"It's like a marriage"—words spoken often by people who have the kind of intense and durable friendships this woman describes. Like the partners in a good marriage, best friends must come to understand how friendship changes, how fears set in, how they continue, without thought, the attempt to reestablish an old equilibrium which, in fact, is forever gone.

For best friendships to survive, the friends must learn to meet today's needs rather than yesterday's, must find ways to reorder the relationship so that it is built on reality rather than illusion. They must be able to tolerate the strain of the changes that inevitably will occur, indeed must welcome them as part of their growth and development, even when they generate some internal conflicts.

Best friends must be able to endure the waxing and waning, the oscillating between periods of closeness and those that are more distant, that is so much a fact of emotional life in intimate relationships. For an emotional mismatch at this level, or one that cannot be corrected, will almost surely doom the friendship. The person who needs some periodic distance will feel overwhelmed by the demands for constant intimacy, while the one who wants always to be close will feel betrayed and abandoned by a friend's wish to take a step away.

Unlike a marriage, however, friendship, in our society, is secured by an emotional bond alone. With no social compact, no ritual moment, no pledge of loyalty and constancy to hold a friendship in place, it becomes not only the most neglected social relationship of our time but, all too often, our most fragile one as well.

Yet at least some friendships, whether best friend or not, are "for life"—a commitment that grows and develops out of the relationship itself, out of a friendship that withstands the test of time, of separation, of togetherness, of uneven levels of development, of uncertain steps toward change, of growth that crawls one moment and gallops the next. In the process, these friendships truly become "like family," combining commitment and obligation with the love that is reserved for *honored* family alone, moving finally from the secular realm to the sacred one.

10

Possibilities

August 21, 1984. It's exactly a year since my friend's son's wedding, a little less than that since I wrote the opening pages of this book. Books, like weddings, open many possibilities. In this instance, the two came together in unexpected ways.

Soon after I wrote them, I gave those pages describing my observations at the wedding to my friend Barbara. "This is just a possibility," I warned. "Obviously I'm not going to publish anything that makes you, Brad or Harriet uncomfortable." A day or so later she called: "I'm very moved by what you wrote. I can't imagine that anyone would object."

I sent them to Brad and his wife, Elana, who, by then, were living on the other side of the country. He phoned: "Reading what you wrote about friends and family was a lesson for me. I never thought about it that way before, but I won't ever be in such a situation again without remembering." "How do you feel about my using it as the opening for the book?" I asked. "I have no objections at all," he replied. "I just don't want to do anything that might hurt Aunt Harriet." "Of course I won't do anything without her full approval," I assured him. "I plan to ask her to read what I've written, but I want to wait until I'm certain I'll use it and know what the context will be."

But Harriet was another matter for me. Barbara is a dear friend; Brad I have known since he was a child—friendships made and kept out of choice, relationships in which we each have a firm sense of what to expect from the other. But like in-laws, Harriet and I have been connected only through her sister. Over the years, we have met at holidays and at significant birthdays, graduations and weddings, always, as Harriet said to me recently, "in a crowd." I couldn't easily predict what she'd feel, how she'd react. So I waited.

Months later, we were together at Barbara's for a holiday dinner. We chatted as we usually do, friendly and warm, but without much substance—until she asked about my work. "I've been hoping you'd ask," I said quickly, trying to cover my anxiety, "because I have an idea for the opening of my friendship book that concerns you." She listened quietly but stiffly, preparing herself for what she might hear.

I told her what I had written about her nephew's wedding, about how I had felt when she was singled out as an honored participant and I was just one of the crowd. When I finished, she said gently, "I guess I can understand how you felt; it makes sense. You and Barbara are so close, and you probably see Brad more than I do."

She turned to her sister, who had joined us a few moments earlier, and asked, "Why didn't you invite Lillian to do that part in the ceremony?" To which Barbara replied somewhat impatiently, "Oh, come on, Harriet, how would you have felt if I had?" "Wait a minute," I interrupted, "that's not the point. The issue isn't why you weren't left out in favor of me, but why I wasn't included along with you, why there isn't enough room at a moment like that for a sister and a best friend who's been as close to the family as I have been?"

The next day I sent Harriet the opening chapter of this book. A few days later she called. "I love it," she said. "Of course you have to publish it; people need to know what's possible in a friendship. Just opening up the subject changed things for us, didn't it? We all know now it wouldn't ever happen that way again. I think it's something people need to think about, and it'll be an eye-opener for them, just as it was for all of us."

Yes, books, like weddings, open many possibilities. For all of us, something that had been, at best, at the periphery of our attention has been brought to its center. In the process, our perceptions have been irrevocably altered, our sense of the appropriate distinctions between friend and kin no longer fixed unthinkingly in custom.

But each book has its own ethos, a strain that runs through the work from start to finish. So I end where I began—with another tale out of my friendship with Barbara, another confrontation with the contradictions and paradox with which this relationship we call "friendship" is charged.

A few days ago, Barbara's mother was celebrating her eightieth birthday with a small "family only" dinner party. Knowing I was sharply limiting all social activities until I finished this book, and wanting to spare me any unnecessary distractions, Barbara defined me out of the family for this occasion—a definition which, this time, I accepted with gratitude. On the day of her birthday, I called Dottie, Barbara's mother, to wish her well. "Why are you calling me?" she demanded. "Aren't you coming to my party tonight?" Startled, I fumbled about, finally saying lamely, "No, I wasn't planning to; I understand it's just the very immediate family." "Well," she countered quickly, "and what are you and Hank?" Then, with exasperation, "I don't understand; I told Barbara and Harriet I want you there. I'll feel terrible if you don't come. You'll be there, won't you?" "Of course," I assured her.

As soon as we rang off, I dialed Barbara's number, relayed to her my conversation with her mother, and agreed that we would be at the dinner that evening. "I'm sorry," she sympathized, "I know how precious your time is right now. But I'm also glad you're coming."

I hung up and sat quietly for a few minutes, thinking about the situation I found myself in, about the feelings I was having. Although I'm very fond of Barbara's mother and was moved by her wish to include my husband and me in her birthday celebration, I felt torn by the pressures of time, by my wish to stay home and write. Yet I knew I *had* to go, just as I would have gone to a similar event in my own family.

"This is what happens when a friendship moves from the secular to the sacred," I said to myself. "This is what it costs. Now I'm not just expected to be responsible to Barbara and her husband and children, but to her mother as well. It's not just a choice anymore; it's an obligation."

"How does it feel?" I asked myself. I wasn't sure; ambivalence encumbered my thoughts. I vacillated between being pleased and touched by this demonstration of the depth and breadth of my friendship with Barbara, of how many lives it had touched and now included, and saying to myself, "Who needs another obligation in this life?" Yet a few hours later, as I sat at the dinner table and looked around me, I wasn't wondering why I was there, wasn't grumbling to myself about still another obligation. Instead, I found myself basking in the warmth of the familiar faces surrounding me, feeling happy to be able to share the moment.

At about the same time all this was going on in my own life, an article entitled "Are Yesterday's Friends Still Friends if Tragedy Strikes?" appeared in *The New York Times.* Written by a woman whose child suddenly fell desperately ill, it tells a bitter tale of friends who disappeared soon after calamity struck.

I was disquieted by the story, felt grieved for this family and the distress their isolation added to their suffering. At the same time, I was mindful of a patient whose child also was felled by a life-threatening illness a few months ago. Like the family in the article, these people, too, have been alternately frightened, angry, unbelieving, depressed and bewildered—certainly not fun-loving, entertaining companions. Yet my patient's friends have been steadfast, forming a circle of support and nurturance that has been the mainstay of their lives in this nightmare through which they are presently living.

"What's the difference?" I wondered. "What kind of life did these other people lead before their child's illness? Who were these so-called friends?" It's hard to know with any certainty, of course. But there are clues in the article—clues that suggest these relationships rested more on what people could *do* together than on how they could *be*, whether, in the author's words, they were "fun to be with," whether they would still be "affluent and well turned out."

Both families are part of the upper middle class, live a life of relative ease; both had believed they could control their destiny, protect their children. But there, I suspect, the similarity ends. My patient has also lived a life of commitment to the public welfare, both wife and husband at least as much concerned for the public good as for private *goods.* In the process, they have gathered around them a community of friends who wouldn't think to notice whether they look "affluent and well turned out."

This community they share doesn't depend on living in the same neighborhood, even in the same city. Rather they are linked together by friendships that are rooted in a shared set of social, political and personal values—deeply held beliefs out of which their commitments to each other have grown. For them, the freedom of choice friendship permits clearly does not also mean freedom from commitment, responsibility and obligation.

Such words have lost popularity, even respectability, in recent years. The restlessness that's expressed in our historic mobility patterns, together with our more recent search for new ways of living our adult years,[1] fits well with those parts of the human potential movement in psychology that have sought to teach us how to find instant intimacy. In a book called *The Temporary Society,* published when optimism about the possibilities of this movement was at its height, two of its leading spokesmen wrote that, in the world they envisioned, we would learn "how to develop intense and deep human relationships quickly—and how to let go" with the same ease.[2] A notion, it seems to me, that is the very antithesis of the humanism it is said to espouse, but perhaps that the friends of the author of the *Times* article learned too well.

The sensitivity training, encounter groups, and their various offshoots, that this movement spawned met with success precisely because they seemed to be responsive to our needs for connection while also permitting us to remain at a comfortable distance from our newfound "friends." In a people who were experiencing disillusion and disaffection with marriage and family life in increasing numbers, who were beginning to question the commitments that had bound former generations to unsatisfactory relationships so tightly, this was seductive stuff indeed. Instant intimacy meant also instant freedom from ties that bind.

But the promise of freedom and safety from the kinds of difficult emotional entanglements we all know so well has turned out to be a frail comfort. Whether among lovers or friends, these disposable relationships have failed to satisfy another set of needs—those that impel us to seek deeper involvement with others, more abiding connections. To meet *these* needs, we will have to find inside us the willingness to become entangled again.

It's not easy in a society where there are no rituals, no social contracts, no shared tasks, no role requirements, no institutional supports of any kind, to bind and hold friends together, to remind them of their responsibilities to one another, of the love they have shared. But if we have learned anything over these recent decades of experimentation with new ways of living, it's that there is no easy way out.

And if this book has taught anything, it is that we need our friends—not just for fun, not just for a replacement for a distant or difficult family or a failed marriage, not just because they can provide the human framework within which we can make good the deficits of the past. All are crucial to our well-being. But we need our friends also because they serve developmental imperatives at every stage of life, because the turning points and transitions that are the inevitable accompaniments of living would be infinitely harder to negotiate without them.

Notes

1. The Neglected Relationship

1. See Bootcheck, 1980, who studied the identity of participants in the wedding ceremony and found that, even here, friends most often substitute for kin when the marriage partner is an only child, when she or he has no same-sex siblings, or when no sibs are geographically available.

2. Many non-Western societies have much more elaborated rituals around the consolidation of a friendship as well as a well developed set of rights and obligations that friends assume toward one another. See, e.g., Brain, 1976, for details of the rituals and obligations surrounding friendship in various non-Western societies where the value of friends is heavily stressed. Among the Bangwa of the Cameroon, for example, in a custom analogous to the arranged marriage, children are given a best friend by their parents, and the friends then assume lifelong commitments and obligations to each other.

3. Reisman and Shorr, 1978, also found that even people who might clearly be considered friendless claim to have some friends.

4. Cf. Block, 1980.

5. The few existing large-scale studies of friendship add to the confusion about how people define friendship and how they feel about their friends. Yankelovich, 1981, p. 251, tells of surveys that "show that 70 percent of Americans now recognize that while they have many acquaintances they have few close friends—and they experience this as a serious void in their lives." But a *Psychology Today* (Parlee, 1979) study analyzing the data from more than 40,000 questionnaires concluded that most people are satisfied with both the quality of their friendships and the number of friends in their lives. Although the results of this study have been widely and correctly criticized because

of the special characteristics of most *Psychology Today* readers and the self-selected sample, no other study of friendship on this scale has been published in the years since it appeared.

Cf. Fischer, 1982, who interviewed over a thousand adults in an effort to determine what people mean when they call someone a friend. His conclusion that "sociability most characterizes associates with the label of 'friend,' intimacy those with the label of 'close,' " is tempered by a warning about the overlap in these categories. In fact, his research shows quite clearly that people called "friend" could also be "close"—meaning, by the definition of this particular research, that they were people with whom confidences were shared, advice sought and money exchanged. Just so, Fischer reminds us, people usually socialized with those who were labeled "close"—whether friend, neighbor or kin. Without careful questioning, then, it's practically impossible to know just what people mean when they call someone a friend.

6. Cf. David Riesman, 1956, who argues that the concern for sociability has bred a nation of "other-directed" conformists.

7. Gordon, 1976. See also Lynch, 1979; Z. Rubin, 1980; Weiss, 1973.

8. Damon, 1977, p. 160.

9. It seems to me evidence of the American bias against friendship as a set of social relations worthy of serious attention that American anthropologists have so little to say on the subject. Yet there's clear evidence that friendships form an important part of the institutionalized social relations in many of the societies they have studied. Cf. Brain, 1976, an Australian anthropologist, who writes about the institutionalization of friendship in non-Western societies.

10. See Poster, 1978, for an excellent analysis of the modern nuclear family and the ways in which it shapes our need for these intense relationships, and also our ambivalence about them.

11. Ibid., p. 170.

12. Weiss, ed., 1973. See also Bensman and Lilienfeld, 1979, for an interesting discussion of the many ways friends help to combat alienation.

13. Garrison, 1978.

14. Wood and Robertson, 1978. Cf. Stueve and Fischer, 1978.

15. Coughey, 1981.

16. See, e.g., Aronson, 1970; Babchuk and Booth, 1969; Bott, 1957; Smith, Form and Stone, 1954; Cantor, 1975; Chrisman, 1970; Fischer et al., 1977; Fischer and Phillips, 1979; Fischer and Oliker, 1980; Jacob-

son, 1970; McGahan, 1972; Litwak and Szelenyi, 1969; Shulman, 1975; Sutcliffe and Crabbe, 1963; Whitten, 1970.

17. See, e.g., Candy, Troll and Levy, 1981; Cott, 1977; Faderman, 1981; Rossi, 1973; Smith-Rosenberg, 1975.

18. To name just a few: "The Friendship Survey," *Esquire* (May 1977); "Friends," *Washington Post Magazine* (June 19, 1977); "Friendship: An Inquiry," *Psychology Today* (March 1979); "The Friendship Bond," *Psychology Today* (October 1979); "Of Male Bondage," *Newsweek* (June 21, 1982); "Focusing on Friends," *New York Times Magazine* (December 4, 1983); "Near and Dear: Friendship and Love Compared," *Psychology Today* (February 1985).

19. Reported in *San Francisco Chronicle,* May 31, 1984.

20. See Hartup, 1976, 1977, 1978; Lever, 1976, 1978; Maas, 1968; Z. Rubin, 1980; Selman and Selman, 1979, on the subject of children's friendships; Douvan and Adelson, 1966; Kagan and Coles, eds., 1972, on adolescent friendships; and on friendships in old age, Blau, 1973; Fischer and Oliker, 1980; Hess, 1979; Riley, Johnson and Foner, 1972; Rosow, 1967.

The realities of our modern era makes friends more important than ever in the conduct and quality of our daily lives. Social and geographic mobility have made kin inaccessible for very large numbers of Americans—always a factor in elevating the status of friendship in any society. Banks, 1972, for example, writes of a Malayan tribe in which economic and population pressures forced migration from the ancestral lands, resulting in the increasing importance of non-kin relationships.

At the same time, the nuclear family has been in trouble. The number of single and divorced adults in our society keeps rising dramatically, while those who continue to live in traditional nuclear families are choosing to have smaller and smaller ones. Where there are no children to take time, attention and emotional energy, the adults are likely to look to friends to fill the gaps. Where there are only one or two children in a family instead of four or five, the chances of establishing a companionable and emotionally supportive relationship with an age mate in the family are greatly reduced. Finally, as we continue to live longer and healthier lives, our needs for companionship and intimacy become increasingly complex—more than can be satisfied in the context of marriage and family alone.

21. Baltes and Schaie, eds., 1973; Block, 1971; Brim and Kagan, 1980; Clarke and Clarke, 1976; Erikson, 1950, 1980; Erikson, ed., 1978; Kagan, 1984; Kegan, 1982; Levinson et al., 1978; Lidz, 1976; Lowen-

thal, Thurnher, Chiriboga, 1975; Maas and Kuypers, 1974; Neugarten, ed., 1968; Rose, ed., 1979; Rosow, 1967; L. Rubin, 1979; Skolnick, 1983b; Thomas and Chess, 1977; Vaillant, 1977.

22. For discussions of this process, see Bowlby, 1969, 1973; Mahler, Pine and Bergman, 1975; Mahler, 1979; Winnicott, 1965a, 1965b.

2. On Kinship and Friendship

1. Cicero, *De Amicitia,* 1898.
2. Burton, *Anatomy of Melancholy,* 1941.
3. Quoted in Diogenes, 1925.
4. Aristotle, Book VIII, Chap. 1
5. Twain, 1964.
6. Emerson, 1951.
7. Bierce, 1979.
8. Eliot, 1958.
9. Jones, ed., 1912.
10. Brain, 1976; Lane, 1980; Radcliffe-Brown, 1950; Schneider, 1968.
11. See, for example, Brain, 1976; Radcliffe-Brown, 1950; Marshall, 1977; Miller and Miller, 1978.
12. Brain, 1976; Radcliffe-Brown, 1950. God parenthood, too, which remains a vital component of family relationships in parts of Catholic Europe and Latin America, is another such socially defined kin relationship.
13. See Ianni, 1971, for an analysis of the structure and function of Mafia families.
14. See Poster, 1978, and Zaretsky, 1976, for excellent critiques of the modern nuclear family; also Sennett, 1970, pp. 184–217, for an interesting discussion of what he calls "the evolution of family intensity" that accompanied the increasing urbanization of American life and the consequent breakdown of the extended family.
15. Frost, 1915.
16. Schneider, 1968.
17. Useem, 1972. See also Finifter, 1974, for an interesting study showing how friendship groups function as supportive environments for political deviants.
18. Cf. Laslett, 1979; Poster, 1978; Skolnick, 1983a.
19. As I have already said, marriage turns stranger into kin. But the family of marriage is, as we all know, much more easily ruptured than is the family of birth. Moreover, when a marriage ends, not just the

nuclear family comes apart but the whole network of in-law relationships usually is disrupted as well, as parents and siblings line up on the sides of their "injured" member. Indeed, when this doesn't happen, the divorcing adults are likely to feel betrayed by what seems to them the disloyalty of their own family.

20. For some major statements of family therapy theory, see Ackerman, 1958; Ackerman, ed., 1970; Bowen, 1978; Erickson and Hogan, eds., 1976; Ferber, Mendelsohn, Napier, eds., 1972; Haley and Hoffman, 1967; Luthman, 1974; Minuchin and Fishman, 1981; Napier and Whitaker, 1978; Neil and Kniskern, eds., 1982; Satir, 1967; Satir, Stachowiak and Taschman, 1975.

3. Many Friends/Many Selves

1. Winnicott, 1971. This is not precisely the meaning Winnicott gives to the concept of "transitional objects." For him, the transitional object is not just the object itself that the child clings to in moments of tension or anxiety—that is, the doll, the blanket, etc.—but the symbolic meaning attributed to the object, the thing that fills the space between the inner and outer worlds, between imagination and reality. My use of the concept is somewhat idiosyncratic but, nevertheless, is an adaptation to the subject of friendship which, it seems to me, remains faithful to the spirit of Winnicott's intent.

2. Douvan and Adelson, 1966; Erikson, 1950; Hartup, 1976, 1977, 1978; Kagan and Coles, eds., 1972; Lever, 1976, 1978; Maas, 1968; Z. Rubin, 1980; Selman and Selman, 1979.

3. There are some class, ethnic and regional differences in the proportion of adults who sustain friendships from childhood or adolescence. Members of working-class ethnic groups, especially in the large eastern cities where social and residential mobility is relatively low, are much more likely than the college-educated middle class to retain friends from the past. But even in this group, the incidence of vital relationships with these old friends is not high, less than one fourth reporting such friendships. See Chapter 6 for further discussion of the ways in which the friends of youth complicate the lives of working-class young marrieds in particular.

4. These identifications are part of what psychoanalysts of the Object Relations School call the internalized objects that make up our inner world. See Balint, ed., 1965; Fairbairn, 1952; Guntrip, 1969; Klein, 1948, 1959; Mahler, Pine and Bergman, 1975; Mahler, 1979; Winnicott, 1965a, 1965b, 1971.

5. Winnicott, 1965b.

6. See, for example, Ainsworth et al., 1978; Bowlby, 1969, 1973, 1980; Klein, 1948, 1959; Kohut, 1977, 1978; Mahler, 1979; Mahler, Pine and Bergman, 1975; Spitz, 1965; Winnicott, 1965a, 1965b, 1971. Even Harry Stack Sullivan, whose emphasis on the importance of interpersonal relations in human development set him in the forefront of psychiatry for his time, missed the implications of his own theory with his insistence that the failure to have a good friend in childhood had lasting deleterious effects on the social adjustment of the adult. For if, as his theory holds, human development is importantly affected by our interpersonal relationships, unless a child is forever isolated from social contact, we cannot assume there will be no corrective experiences along the way.

7. I refer here to the theorists of the Object Relations School in both Great Britain and the United States. Op. cit., note 4 above.

8. See, for example, Brim and Kagan, 1980; Clarke and Clarke, 1976; Kagan, 1984; Kagan, Kearsley and Zelazo, 1978; Kegan, 1982; Skolnick 1983b; Thomas and Chess, 1977.

9. My thanks to Diane Ehrensaft, whose many conversations with me about the developmental implications of the work I have been doing were extremely helpful, and who, in the course of one of those discussions, shared with me this metaphor of the tapestry.

10. Goffman, 1963.

11. I interviewed two pairs of twins—one male, one female— and two women who were each half of a twin set.

4. Men, Women and Friends: The Differences Between Us

1. Tiger, 1969.

2. Bacon, 1937.

3. Taylor, 1913.

4. Smith-Rosenberg, 1975. See also Bernikow, 1980; Cott, 1977; Faderman, 1981; Rossi, 1973.

5. Balswick and Peek, 1971; David and Brannon, eds., 1976; Farrell, 1975; Fasteau, 1975; Fischer and Narus, 1981; Jacoby, 1978; Jourard, 1971; Komarovsky, 1976; Lewis, 1978; Miller, 1983; O'Leary and Donoghue, 1978; Pleck, 1975, 1981; Pleck and Brannon, eds., 1978; Pleck and Sawyer, eds., 1974; Robertiello, 1979; L. Rubin, 1983; Sattel, 1976.

6. Michaels, 1982.

7. Levinson et al., 1978, p. 335.

8. Engel, 1982.

9. I refer only to friendships among heterosexual men and women, since the friendships of homosexual men and lesbians are different enough both from each other and from those of their straight sisters and brothers as to require a separate discussion.

10. Fischer and Oliker, 1980.

11. Fischer et al., 1977; Fischer and Oliker, 1980; Stueve and Gerson, 1977.

12. Abel, 1981; Bell, 1981a, 1981b; Bernard, 1981; Bernikow, 1980; Blau, 1973; Block, 1980; Booth, 1972; Candy, Troll and Levy, 1981; Cott, 1977; Davidson and Duberman, 1979; Faderman, 1981; Fischer and Narus, 1981; Hess, 1976, 1979; Lowenthal and Haven, 1968; Mark and Alper, 1980; Powers and Bultena, 1976; Seiden and Bart, 1975; Smith-Rosenberg, 1975; Weiss and Lowenthal, 1975

13. Balswick and Avertt, 1977; Balswick and Peek, 1971; Bell, 1981a, 1981b; Block, 1980; Booth, 1972; Booth and Hess, 1974; Cicone and Ruble, 1978; Fischer and Narus, 1981; Hill and Stull, 1981; Jacoby, 1978; Jourard, 1971; Komarovsky, 1974, 1976; Lewis, 1978; Mark and Alper, 1980; Michaels, 1982; Miller, 1983; Morin and Garfinkle, 1978; Pleck, 1975, 1981; Powers and Bultena, 1976; Weiss and Lowenthal, 1975.

14. I use the term "bonding" as distinct from "attachment," which, in the psychoanalytic literature, has a particular meaning that generally denotes a relationship where the level of security of one person depends upon the predictable availability of the other—e.g., mother-infant, husband-wife. Bonding, as I am using it here, refers to an emotional connection that is unrelated to the internal security needs of the individuals involved and does not *require* the immediate presence of the other.

15. Brain, 1976, pp. 68–74.

16. Mead, 1955, p. 214.

17. Haley, in press.

5. Understanding Our Differences

1. Z. Rubin, 1980, p. 106.

2. Douvan and Adelson, 1966, pp. 201–202.

3. Lever, 1976, 1978.

4. See Ibid. for an excellent analysis of how the different childhood play experiences of boys and girls become training for their sex-stereotyped adult roles.

5. Ibid., p. 485.
6. Chodorow, 1978, whose theoretical formulations about the development of stereotypic gender identity and behavior are the starting point for my own work. Cf. also Dinnerstein, 1976.
7. What follows is an all too brief synopsis of the theory presented in my book *Intimate Strangers,* 1983. There I show not only how the differences in male and female personality structures arise, but also how these differences affect such critical issues in adult relationships as intimacy, sexuality, dependency, work and parenting.
8. These theoretical shifts started with the British Object Relations School, who came to see the importance of the pre-Oedipal period in the development of the child (Op. cit., Chapter 3, note 4), and culminated in Chodorow's, 1978, reformulation of the developmental differences between girls and boys. See L. Rubin, 1983, for an analysis of how these new theoretical formulations help us to understand the behavioral differences between men and women that are so common in our society.
9. The *Encyclopedia of Psychoanalysis* (Eidelberg, ed., 1968) defines symbiosis as "denotative of a biological condition in which two subjects live in a close spatial and physiologically reciprocal dependent relationship."
10. Kohut, 1977, 1978.
11. Miller, 1983, p. 2. See also Chesler, 1978, for an interesting analysis of the sources of homophobia in men.

As with the other disciplines dealing with human behavior and psychology, the literature of classical psychoanalytic theory, which has so powerfully influenced the twentieth-century world view, has almost nothing to say about friendship. In the only article in the psychoanalytic literature to examine friendship over the last two decades, the author argues that friendship (by which we must assume he means male friendships, since women's friendships are nowhere mentioned) is based on the repression of the sexual drive, which then imperils friendship whenever the repressed material threatens to break through into consciousness. By being aim-inhibited, friendships, he concludes, "define the fate of the homosexual instinctual stream (Rangell, 1963, p. 51)."

12. Miller, 1983, p. 3.
13. Ibid.
14. Cf. Gilligan, 1982, who has written persuasively about the origins of such differences between boys and girls. In her study, adolescent children were asked to resolve a dilemma in which a man consid-

ers whether or not to steal a drug he cannot afford to buy in order to save his wife's life. In analyzing the differences in the children's responses, Gilligan found that for the boys, formal, legalistic logic and abstract notions of equity and fairness controlled their decision; for the girls, relationships and the context within which they were embedded were the focus of their concern.

15. My thanks to Karen Paige for these evocative terms.

6. From Singles to Couples and Back Again: A Rocky Road for Friends

1. See Z. Rubin, 1980, for a fuller discussion of children's friendships and their functions; also Serbin, Tonick and Sternglanz, 1977, for a study that sought to shape and encourage cross-sex play among nursery-school children and found that play between girls and boys increased dramatically when teachers commented approvingly about it within hearing of the entire class.

2. Cf. Douvan and Adelson, 1966, for a classic analysis of adolescent friendships.

3. Selman and Selman, 1979.

4. L. Rubin, 1976. See also Allan, 1977; Bott, 1957; Gans, 1965; Komarovsky, 1962; Kornblum, 1974; Shostak, 1969; Sennett and Cobb, 1973; Young and Willmott, 1962.

5. See Joffe, 1977, for an analysis of the class-related issues that lie at the heart of much of the controversy around early childhood education; also L. Rubin, 1972 and 1976, pp. 85–87, which argues that most working-class parents are either uncertain about or downright antagonistic to the middle-class values that dominate most American child care institutions.

6. See also Babchuk, 1965; Babchuck and Bates, 1963; Lopata, 1971, 1975, for discussions of what Lopata calls "couple-companionate relations."

7. For more about the social relationships of the never-married, divorced and widowed, see Adams, 1976; Bequaert, 1976; Bohannon, ed., 1971; Cauhapé, 1983; Epstein, 1974; Goode, 1956; Hiltz, 1981; Lopata, 1973, 1979; Lynch, 1979; Stein, ed., 1981; Weiss, 1975, 1979; Weiss, ed., 1973.

8. While women have made some gains to equalize power with men in the formal and legal structures (the equal pay for equal work laws, for example), at the more informal levels of social life, the clock, if anything, may have moved backward. Cf. Ehrenreich, 1983, who

makes a persuasive argument about the "collapse of the breadwinner ethic" and with it, men's flight from commitment to marriage and the family.

One of the more obvious, albeit unattended, ways men continue to have more power in their relationships with women (even when incomes are equal or close to it) is the difference in the way this society views an aging woman and an aging man. The potential for remarriage of the forty-year-old divorcée, for example, is very slim when compared to her forty-three-year-old ex-husband. He has no trouble finding a woman considerably younger than himself to share his bed and his paycheck, while his ex-wife will either marry a sixty-year-old or, more likely, live the rest of her life without a man around the house. Indeed, the statistics on male remarriage show quite clearly that, while more men than ever before may do the dishes occasionally, they're more likely to be doing them in a household where the wife is ten, twenty, even thirty years younger than her husband.

9. The issue of who pays is often also a delicate matter when the single friend is a woman. When she joins a couple for some activity outside the home, the man may feel awkward about accepting her money, and at the same time, wife and husband probably will be resentful of the extra expense. Thus, even when a woman is very careful about holding up her financial end, the couple may decide it's just easier not to have to face the discomfort the situation engenders.

7. On Marriage and Friendship

1. The ages I mention here refer to the majority of people whose life cycle time clock matches the norms. While still a small statistical minority, there are today a substantial number of couples who are marrying much later and having their first child well into their thirties and early forties. The friendship patterns of these couples will probably differ somewhat from those I have laid out here since their age and stage in the family life cycle do not match those of the majority of the population.

Although there were too few such people in the sample to allow any firm statements, those I met suggest that such couples already live among others who also deviate from the age norms, since most women who delay childbearing for so long are professionals whose closest friends are others like themselves. Where this is not the case, they will meet and make friends (whether in pregnancy and birth classes or around the activities of parents of infants and very young children) with couples who are substantially younger than they are, in order to share with them the joys and problems of the early childbearing and childrearing years.

What will happen to old friends who are at a clearly different life stage is an open question. But I would speculate that their relationship would wane through the early years of childrearing, and in those cases where the original bonds were strong enough to tolerate a prolonged attenuation of the friendship, would wax again as the children grow. Throughout the rest of their lives, however, the people who have delayed childbearing probably will move in a mixed circle of friends, going to the confirmations of those who are their children's playmates and classmates when they go to the weddings of the children of other friends.

2. See L. Rubin, 1983, especially Chapters 3–8, for an analysis of this separation-unity theme as it affects our marriage relationships; cf. Benjamin, 1980; Chodorow, 1978; Dinnerstein, 1976.

3. For other discussions and analyses of the paucity of friendships among adult men, Balswick and Peek, 1971; Bell, 1981a, 1981b; Block, 1980; Booth and Hess, 1974; Cicone and Ruble, 1978; Fischer and Narus, 1981; Jacoby, 1978; Jourard, 1971; Komarovsky, 1974, 1976; Levinson et al., 1978; Lewis, 1978; Mark and Alper, 1980; Michaels, 1982; Miller, 1983; Morin and Garfinkle, 1978; Pleck, 1975, 1981; Powers and Bultena, 1976; Weiss and Lowenthal, 1975.

4. Cf. Evans and Bartolomé, 1981; Rohrlich, 1980; L. Rubin, 1979.

8. Women and Men as Friends: Mind, Body and Emotion

1. Forty-two percent of the heterosexual men and 34 percent of the women said they had close friends of the opposite sex. Cf. Booth and Hess, 1974, who surveyed 800 adults aged 45 and over and found that 35 percent of the men and 24 percent of the women had close opposite-sex friends. The disparity between their findings and mine may be accounted for by the older age of their respondents, since there is some evidence that cross-sex friendships are likely to be most common in a younger population.

Bell, 1981a, reports findings that differ substantially from mine and those of Booth and Hess. In his study, 10 percent of the women and 34 percent of the men reported no close friendships with members of the opposite sex. Since Bell does not give any information about the age or status of his sample, except to say that "none of them was a complete stranger to me" (p. 27), it is impossible even to speculate about how to account for these differences.

2. Obviously many of the issues that arise in cross-sex friendships in the straight world are felt in same-sex friendships among lesbians and gay men. But the complications of these friendships among gays are large enough to deserve separate treatment. Therefore, this chapter will deal with heterosexual men and women only.

3. Cf. Safilios-Rothschild, 1977, who also suggests that, when sexual tension and incompatibility is one cause of a couple's problems, a friendship can be better after the sexual relationship ends.

4. For some discussion about changing sexual norms and the conflicts they create, see Bell, 1966; Blumstein and Schwartz, 1983; Gagnon and Simon, 1974; Hite, 1976; Laws and Schwartz, 1977; Pietropinto and Simenauer, 1981; L. Rubin, 1976, 1979, 1983; Sherfey, 1973; Zilbergeld, 1978.

5. Although the number of couples not married but living together in a committed relationship in this research is too small to allow any sweeping generalizations, among the people I interviewed, there was little difference between them and the marrieds when class and age were comparable.

6. Cf. Bell, 1981a, 1981b; Booth and Hess, 1974, for studies showing similar findings.

7. Cf. Booth and Hess, 1974.

8. Cf. Bell, 1981a, Chapter 5; Komarovsky, 1974, 1976; Michaels, 1982; Miller, 1983; Pleck, 1975.

9. Cf. Bernikow, 1980; Cott, 1977; Smith-Rosenberg, 1975.

10. Gilligan, 1982.

11. West, 1984, presents empirical evidence showing that patients respond dramatically differently to the authority of a female and a male physician. Basing her findings on a detailed analysis of videotaped encounters, she shows that "physicians interrupt patients disproportionately—*except* when the doctor is a 'lady.' Then, patients interrupt as much or more than physicians, and their interruptions seem to subvert the physicians' authority (pp. 87–88)." [*Emphasis in the original.*] Although the sample in this article is too small to permit any generalizations, the data are unequivocal in showing that male patients interrupt a woman physician *far more often* than they interrupt a man.

12. Bell and Weinberg, 1978.

13. Cf. Malone, 1980, p. 9, who also notes that among the 150 gay men he interviewed, "almost all were friendly with many more straight women than lesbians."

14. Ibid., p. 4.

15. While these observations are certainly apt, there are also social and political issues that divide homosexual men and lesbians. The life style of a high proportion of homosexual men differs markedly from the preferred mode of most lesbians, with the women often wanting to distance themselves from the more flamboyant and promiscuous image that attaches to male homosexual life. Also, paradoxically, while gay women and men have been drawn together in a common political cause, they find themselves in competition for the scarce resources their movement has opened up. Thus in a city like San Francisco, where the homosexual population is large enough to have developed some political clout, gay male and lesbian groups often find themselves in an uncomfortable and unwanted competitive situation that bodes ill for easy friendships between them.

16. The other male-female friendships that I have not mentioned here—those between an older woman and a younger man—are also generally free of many of the traditional tensions I have discussed in this chapter. Like the gay/straight friendships, these, too, are not usually greatly burdened by sexual tensions since an older woman in this society is not thought of as an appropriate or desirable sexual partner. Moreover, most of the women who talked about these friendships said that they often have enough of the mother-son relationship embedded in them so that the woman does not feel disadvantaged in the balance of power in the friendship, as she might with a man who is an age peer.

9. Best Friends

1. See Chapter 4, "Men, Women and Friends," pp. 59–79, for differences in the proportions of women and men who could name a best friend.

2. Weiss, ed., 1973, argues that to counteract loneliness it is less important to be in the physical presence of a loved one than to know that she or he will be there when needed. But although the people I am speaking of here *say* they believe the friend would be there if and when needed, there's no evidence to suggest that this is anything more than a fantasy, since the relationships they describe are not with loved

ones, nor are they the kinds of friendships that could reasonably support such an expectation.

3. Klein, 1948, 1959.

10. Possibilities

1. These new aspirations for adulthood and for adult relationships are not simply a product of the "new narcissism," as some critics have charged. Rather, they are a response to a new set of social forces, not least of them the medical technology that has dramatically lengthened our life span while, at the same time, facilitating a markedly lower birthrate. Together, these changes mean that, for the first time in history, we now live a substantial number of adult years after our childrearing responsibilities are done, leading us, I believe, to the "discovery" of adulthood in this era as a stage of life with its own developmental potential.

When, as in earlier eras, adult life ended soon after the last child was launched, there was little concern about adulthood and its relationships. Now that this is no longer the case, we find ourselves thinking about how we will live these years in satisfactory ways—about whether the relationships we bring to them can meet the new challenge, about how we can ensure the intimacy and companionship within them to enrich this period of our lives, even whether the work we undertook at twenty or twenty-five still fits at forty-five, given that we can look forward to twenty-five or thirty more active years.

2. Bennis and Slater, 1968, p. 127.

Bibliography

Abel, Elizabeth. "(E)merging Identities: The Dynamics of Female Friendship in Contemporary Fiction by Women." *Signs* 6 (1981), pp. 413–435.

Ackerman, Nathan W. *The Psychodynamics of Family Life.* New York: Basic Books, 1958.

———, ed. *Family Process.* New York: Basic Books, 1970.

Adams, Margaret. *Single Blessedness.* New York: Basic Books, 1976.

Ainsworth, Mary D. S., et al. *Patterns of Attachment.* Hillsdale, N.J.: Lawrence Erlbaum Associates, 1978.

Allan, Graham. "Class Variations in Friendship Patterns." *British Journal of Sociology* 28 (1977), pp. 389–393.

Aristotle. *The Ethics of Aristotle: The Nichomachean Ethics.* Revised edition. Translated by J. A. K. Thomson. Harmondsworth, England: Penguin Books, 1976.

Aronson, Dan R. "Social Networks: Towards Structure or Process?" *Canadian Review of Sociology and Anthropology* 7 (1970), pp. 258–268.

Babchuk, Nicholas. "Primary Friends and Kin: A Study of the Association of Middle-Class Couples." *Social Forces* 43 (1965), pp. 483–493.

———, and Alan P. Bates. "The Primary Relations of Middle-Class Couples: A Study in Male Dominance." *American Sociological Review* 28 (1963), pp. 377–384.

———, and Alan Booth. "Voluntary Association Membership: A Longitudinal Analysis." *American Sociological Review* 34 (1969), pp. 31–45.

Bacon, Sir Francis. "On Friendship." *Essays, Advancement of Learning, New Atlantis, and Other Pieces.* New York: Odyssey Press, 1937.

Balint, Michael, ed. *Primary Love and Psycho-Analytic Technique.* New York: Liveright, 1965.

Balswick, Jack, and Christine Proctor Avertt. "Differences in Expressiveness: Gender, Interpersonal Orientation, and Perceived Parental Expressiveness as Contributing Factors." *Journal of Marriage and the Family* 39 (1977), pp. 121–127.

———, and Charles Peek. "The Inexpressive Male: A Tragedy of American Society." *The Family Coordinator* 20 (1971), pp. 363–368.

Baltes, Paul B., and K. Warner Schaie, eds. *Life-Span Developmental Psychology.* New York: Academic Press, 1973.

Banks, David J. "Changing Kinship in North Malaya." *American Anthropologist* 74 (1972), pp. 1254–1275.

Bell, Alan P., and Martin S. Weinberg. *Homosexualities: A Study of Diversity Among Men and Women.* New York: Simon and Schuster, 1978.

Bell, Robert R. *Premarital Sex in a Changing Society.* Englewood Cliffs, N.J.: Prentice-Hall, 1966.

———. *Worlds of Friendship.* Beverly Hills: Sage Publications, 1981a.

———. "Friendships of Women and of Men." *Psychology of Women Quarterly* 5 (1981b), pp. 402–417.

Benjamin, Jessica. "The Bonds of Love: Rational Violence and Erotic Domination." *Feminist Studies* 6 (1980), pp. 144–174.

Bennis, Warren, and Philip Slater. *The Temporary Society.* New York: Harper Colophon, 1968.

Bensman, Joseph, and Robert Lilienfeld. "Friendship and Alienation." *Psychology Today* 13 (1979), pp. 56–66, 114.

Bequaert, Lucia H. *Single Women: Alone and Together.* Boston: Beacon Press, 1976.

Bernard, Jessie. *The Female World.* New York: Free Press, 1981.

Bernikow, Louise. *Among Women.* New York: Harmony Books, 1980.

Bierce, Ambrose. *The Devil's Dictionary.* New York: T. Y. Crowell, 1979.

Blau, Zena Smith. *Old Age in a Changing Society.* New York: New Viewpoints, 1973.

Block, Jack. *Lives Through Time.* Berkeley: Bancroft Books, 1971.

Block, Joel D. *Friendship.* New York: Macmillan, 1980.

Blumstein, Philip, and Pepper Schwartz. *American Couples: Money, Work, Sex.* New York: William Morrow, 1983.

Bohannon, Paul, ed. *Divorce and After.* Garden City, N.Y.: Anchor Books, 1971.

Bootcheck, Judith A. "Kinship and Friendship: A Substitutability Hypothesis." Unpublished paper presented to the Annual Meetings of the Illinois Sociological Association, 1980.

Booth, Alan. "Sex and Social Participation." *American Sociological Review* 37 (1972), pp. 183–192.

———, and Elaine Hess. "Cross-Sex Friendships." *Journal of Marriage and the Family* 36 (1974), pp. 38–47.

Bott, Elizabeth. *Family and Social Network: Roles, Norms and External Relationships in Ordinary Urban Families.* London: Tavistock Publications, 1957.

Bowen, Murray. *Family Therapy in Clinical Practice.* New York: Jason Aronson, 1978.

Bowlby, John. *Attachment.* New York: Basic Books, 1969.

———. *Separation.* New York: Basic Books, 1973.

———. *Loss: Sadness and Despair.* New York: Basic Books, 1980.

Brain, Robert. *Friends and Lovers.* New York: Basic Books, 1976.

Brim, Orville R., and Jerome Kagan. *Constancy and Change in Human Development.* Cambridge: Harvard University Press, 1980.

Burton, Robert. *Anatomy of Melancholy.* New York: Tudor Publishing, 1941.

Candy, Sandra Gibbs, Lillian E. Troll and Sheldon G. Levy. "A Developmental Exploration of Friendship Functions in Women." *Psychology of Women Quarterly* 5 (1981), pp. 456–472.

Cantor, Marjorie H. "Life Space and the Social Support System of the Inner City Elderly of New York." *Gerontologist* 15 (1975), pp. 23–27.

Cauhapé, Elizabeth. *Fresh Starts.* New York: Basic Books, 1983.

Chesler, Phyllis. *About Men.* New York: Simon and Schuster, 1978.

Chodorow, Nancy. *The Reproduction of Mothering: Psychoanalysis and the Sociology of Gender.* Berkeley: University of California Press, 1978.

Chrisman, Noel J. "Situation and the Social Network in Cities." *Canadian Review of Sociology and Anthropology* 7 (1970), pp. 245–257.

Cicero, Marcus Tullius. *De Amicitia.* New York: Century Company, 1898.

Cicone, Michael V., and Diane N. Ruble. "Beliefs About Males." *Journal of Social Issues* 34 (1978), pp. 5–16.

Clarke, Ann Margaret, and Alan D. B. Clarke. *Early Experience: Myth and Evidence.* New York: Free Press, 1976.

Cott, Nancy F. *Bonds of Womanhood.* New Haven: Yale University Press, 1977.

Coughey, Kathleen. "Divorced But Not Alone: A Study of Divorced Women's Social Networks." Unpublished paper presented to the Annual Meetings of the Society for the Study of Social Problems, 1981.

Damon, William. *The Social World of the Child.* San Francisco: Jossey-Bass, 1977.

David, Deborah S., and Robert Brannon, eds. *The Forty-Nine Percent Majority: The Male Sex Role.* Menlo Park, Calif.: Addison-Wesley, 1976.

Davidson, Lynne R., and Lucille Duberman. "Same-Sex Friendships: A Gender Comparison of Dyads." Unpublished paper presented to the Annual Meetings of the American Sociological Association, 1979.

Davis, Keith E. "Near and Dear: Friendship and Love Compared." *Psychology Today* 19 (1985), pp. 22–30.

Dinnerstein, Dorothy. *The Mermaid and the Minotaur.* New York: Harper & Row, 1976.

Diogenes, Laertius. *Lives of Eminent Philosophers.* Translated by R. D. Hicks. New York: G. P. Putnam, 1925.

Douvan, Elizabeth, and Joseph Adelson. *The Adolescent Experience.* New York: John Wiley, 1966.

Ehrenreich, Barbara. *The Hearts of Men.* Garden City, N. Y.: Anchor Press/Doubleday, 1983.

Eidelberg, Ludwig, ed. *Encyclopedia of Psychoanalysis.* New York: Free Press, 1968.

Eliot, T. S. *The Elder Statesman.* London: Faber and Faber, 1969.

Emerson, Ralph Waldo. "Friendship." *Essays.* New York: Thomas Y. Crowell, 1951.

Engel, Elliot. "Of Male Bondage." *Newsweek* 99 (1982), p. 13.

Epstein, Joseph. *Divorced in America.* New York: Penguin Books, 1974.

Erickson, Gerald D., and Terrence P. Hogan, eds. *Family Therapy.* New York: Jason Aronson, 1976.

Erikson, Erik H. *Childhood and Society.* New York: W. W. Norton, 1950.

———. *Identity and the Life Cycle.* New York: W. W. Norton, 1980.

———, ed. *Adulthood.* New York: W. W. Norton, 1978.

Evans, Paul, and Fernando Bartolomé. *Must Success Cost So Much?* New York: Basic Books, 1981.

Faderman, Lillian. *Surpassing the Love of Men.* New York: William Morrow, 1981.

Fairbairn, W. R. D. *An Object Relations Theory of Personality.* New York: Basic Books, 1952.

Farrell, Warren. *The Liberated Man.* New York: Bantam Books, 1975.

Fasteau, Marc Feigen. *The Male Machine.* New York: Delta Books, 1975.

Ferber, Andrew, Marilyn Mendelsohn, Augustus Napier, eds. *The Book of Family Therapy.* New York: Science House, 1972.

Finifter, Ada W. "The Friendship Group as a Protective Environment for Political Deviants." *American Political Science Review* 68 (1974), pp. 607–625.

Fischer, Claude S. "What Do We Mean by 'Friend'?" *Social Networks* 3 (1982), pp. 287–306.

———, et al. *Networks and Places: Social Relations in the Urban Setting.* New York: Free Press, 1977.

———, and Susan L. Phillips. "Who Is Alone? Social Characteristics of People with Small Networks." Working Paper No. 31 (1979). Institute of Urban and Regional Development, University of California, Berkeley.

———, and Stacey J. Oliker. "Friendship, Sex and the Life Cycle." Working Paper No. 318 (1980). Institute of Urban and Regional Development, University of California, Berkeley.

Fischer, Judith L., and Leonard R. Narus, Jr. "Sex Roles and Intimacy in Same Sex and Other Sex Relationships." *Psychology of Women Quarterly* 5 (1981), pp. 444–455.

Frost, Robert. "The Death of the Hired Man." *North of Boston.* Second edition. New York: H. Holt, 1915.

Gagnon, John H., and William Simon. *Sexual Conduct: The Social Sources of Human Sexuality.* Chicago: Aldine, 1974.

Gans, Herbert J. *The Urban Villagers.* New York: Free Press, 1965.

Garrison, Vivian. "Support System of Schizophrenic and Nonschizophrenic Puerto Rican Migrant Women in New York City." *Schizophrenia Bulletin* 4 (1978), pp. 561–596.

Gilligan, Carol. *In a Different Voice: Psychological Theory and Women's Development.* Cambridge, Mass.: Harvard University Press, 1982.

Goffman, Erving. *Stigma.* Englewood Cliffs, N.J.: Prentice-Hall, 1963.

Goode, William J. *Women in Divorce.* New York: Free Press, 1956.

Gordon, Suzanne. *Lonely in America.* New York: Simon and Schuster, 1976.

Guntrip, Harry. *Schizoid Phenomena, Object Relations and the Self.* New York: International Universities Press, 1969.

Haley, Jay, and Lynn Hoffman. *Techniques of Family Therapy.* New York: Basic Books, 1967.

Haley, Sarah A. "Some of My Best Friends Are Dead." In William E. Kelley, ed. *Post-Traumatic Stress Disorder and the War Veteran Patient.* New York: Brunner/Mazel, in press.

Hartup, Willard W. "Peer Interaction and the Behavioral Development of the Individual Child." In Eric Schopler and Robert J. Reichler, eds. *Psychopathology and Child Development.* New York: Plenum, 1976.

———. "Peers, Play and Pathology: A New Look at the Social Behavior of Children." *Newsletter.* Society for Research in Child Development (1977), pp. 1–3.

———. "Peer Relations and the Processes of Socialization." In Michael T. Guralnick, ed. *Early Intervention and the Integration of Handicapped and Nonhandicapped Children.* Baltimore: University Park Press, 1978.

Hess, Beth B. "Sex Roles, Friendship and the Life Course." *Research on Aging* 1 (1979), pp. 494–515.

———. "Friendship and Gender Roles Over the Life Course." In Peter J. Stein, ed. *Single Life.* New York: St. Martin's Press, 1981.

Hill, Charles T., and Donald E. Stull. "Sex Differences in Effects of Social Value Similarity in Same-Sex Friendship." *Journal of Personality and Social Psychology* 41 (1981), pp. 488–502.

Hiltz, Starr Roxanne. "Widowhood: A Roleless Role." In Peter J. Stein, ed. *Single Life.* New York: St. Martin's Press, 1981.

Hite, Shere. *The Hite Report.* New York: Dell, 1976.

Ianni, Francis A. J. "The Mafia and the Web of Kinship." *Public Interest* 22 (1971), pp. 78–100.

Jacobson, David. "Network Analysis in East Africa: The Social Organization of Urban Transients." *Canadian Review of Sociology and Anthropology* 7 (1970), pp. 281–286.

Jacoby, Susan. "Emotional Intimacy: Are Men Asking Too Much?" *McCall's* 106 (1978), pp. 138, 210–214.

Joffe, Carole E. *Friendly Intruders: Childcare Professionals and Family Life.* Berkeley: University of California Press, 1977.

Jones, Henry Festing, ed. *Notebooks of Samuel Butler.* London: A. C. Fifeld, 1912.

Jourard, Sidney M. *The Transparent Self.* New York: D. Van Nostrand, 1971.

Kagan, Jerome. *The Nature of the Child.* New York: Basic Books, 1984.

———, Richard B. Kearsley and Philip R. Zelazo. *Infancy: Its Place in Human Development.* Cambridge, Mass.: Harvard University Press, 1978.

———, and Robert Coles, eds. *From Twelve to Sixteen: Early Adolescence.* New York: W. W. Norton, 1972.

Kegan, Robert. *The Evolving Self: Problem and Process in Human Development.* Cambridge, Mass.: Harvard University Press, 1982.

Klein, Melanie. *Contributions to Psycho-Analysis.* London: Hogarth Press, 1948.

———. *The Psycho-Analysis of Children.* London: Hogarth Press, 1959.

Kohut, Heinz. *The Restoration of the Self.* New York: International Universities Press, 1977.

———. *The Search for Self.* Vols. 1 and 2. New York: International Universities Press, 1978.

Komarovsky, Mirra. *Blue-Collar Marriage.* New York: Vintage Books, 1962.

———. "Patterns of Self-Disclosure of Male Undergraduates." *Journal of Marriage and the Family* 36 (1974), pp. 677–686.

———. *Dilemmas of Masculinity.* New York: W. W. Norton, 1976.

Kornblum, William. *Blue Collar Community.* Chicago: University of Chicago Press, 1974.

Kurth, Suzanne B. "Friendships and Friendly Relations." In George J. McCall, Norman Denzin, Suzanne B. Kurth, eds. *Social Relationships.* Chicago: Aldine, 1970.

Lane, Warren. "Classical Moral Paradigms and the Meaning of Kinship: A Philosophical Examination." *Dialectical Anthropology* 5 (1980), pp. 193–214.

Laslett, Barbara. "The Significance of Family Membership." In Virginia Tufte and Barbara Myerhoff, eds. *Changing Images of the Family.* New Haven: Yale University Press, 1979.

Laws, Judith Long, and Pepper Schwartz. *Sexual Scripts: The Social Construction of Female Sexuality.* Hinsdale, Ill.: Dryden Press, 1977.

Lazarsfeld, Paul F., and Robert K. Merton. "Friendship as a Social Process: A Substantive and Methodological Analysis." In Monroe Berger, Theodore Abel and Charles H. Page, eds. *Freedom and Control in Modern Society.* New York: D. Van Nostrand, 1964.

Lever, Janet. "Sex Differences in the Games Children Play." *Social Problems* 23 (1976), pp. 478–487.

———. "Sex Differences in the Complexity of Children's Play." *American Sociological Review* 43 (1978), pp. 471–483.

Levinson, Daniel J., et al. *The Seasons of a Man's Life.* New York: Alfred A. Knopf, 1978.

Lewis, Robert A. "Emotional Intimacy Among Men." *Journal of Social Issues* 34 (1978), pp. 108–121.

Lidz, Theodore. *The Person.* Revised edition. New York: Basic Books, 1976.

Lieberman, Alicia F. "Preschoolers' Competence with a Peer: Influence of Attachment and Social Experience." *Child Development* 48 (1977), pp. 1277–1287.

Litwak, Eugene, and Ivan Szelenyi. "Primary Group Structures and their Functions: Kin, Neighbors and Friends." *American Sociological Review* 34 (1969), pp. 465–481.

Lopata, Helena Znaniecki. *Occupation Housewife.* New York: Oxford University Press, 1971.

———. "Couple-Companionate Relationships in Marriage and Widowhood." In Nona Glazer-Malbin, ed., *Old Family/New Family.* New York: D. Van Nostrand, 1975.

———. *Widowhood in an American City.* Cambridge, Mass.: Schenkman, 1973.

———. *Women as Widows.* New York: Elsevier, 1979.

Lowenthal, Marjorie Fiske, Majda Thurnher, David Chiriboga. *Four Stages of Life.* San Francisco: Jossey-Bass, 1975.

———, and Clayton Haven. "Interaction and Adaptation: Intimacy as a Critical Variable." *American Sociological Review* 33 (1968), pp. 20–30.

———, and Lawrence Weiss. "Intimacy and Crisis in Adulthood." *The Counseling Psychologist* 6 (1976), pp. 10–15.

Luthman, Shirley Gehrke. *The Dynamic Family.* Palo Alto: Science and Behavior Books, 1974.

Lynch, James J. *The Broken Heart: The Medical Consequences of Loneliness.* New York: Basic/Harper Colophon, 1979.

Maas, Henry S. "Preadolescent Peer Relations and Adult Intimacy." *Psychiatry* 31 (1968), pp. 161–172.

———, and Joseph A. Kuypers. *From Thirty to Seventy.* San Francisco: Jossey-Bass, 1974.

Macionis, John J. "Intimacy: Structure and Process in Interpersonal Relationships." *Alternative Lifestyles* 1 (1978), pp. 113–130.

McGahan, Peter. "The Neighbor Role and Neighboring in a Highly Urban Area." *Sociological Quarterly* 13 (1972), pp. 397–408.

Mahler, Margaret S. *Separation-Individuation.* New York: Jason Aronson, 1979.

———, Fred Pine and Anni Bergman. *The Psychological Birth of the Human Infant.* New York: Basic Books, 1975.

Malone, John. *Straight Women/Gay Men.* New York: Dial Press, 1980.

Mark, Elizabeth Wyner, and Thelma G. Alper. "Sex Role Differences in Intimacy Motivation." *Psychology of Women Quarterly* 5 (1980), pp. 164–169.

Marshall, Mac. "The Nature of Nurture." *American Ethnologist* 4 (1977), pp. 643–662.

Mead, Margaret. *Male and Female.* New York: New American Library, 1955.

Michaels, Leonard. *The Men's Club.* New York: Avon, 1982.

Miller, Roy A., and Maria G. Miller. "The Golden Chain: A Study of the Structure, Function and Patterning of Co-Parenting in a South Italian Village." *American Ethnologist* 5 (1978), pp. 116–136.

Miller, Stuart. *Men and Friendship.* Boston: Houghton Mifflin, 1983.

Minuchin, Salvador, and H. Charles Fishman. *Family Therapy Techniques.* Cambridge, Mass.: Harvard University Press, 1981.

Morin, Stephen F., and Ellen M. Garfinkle. "Male Homophobia." *Journal of Social Issues* 34 (1978), pp. 29–47.

Napier, Augustus Y., and Carl A. Whitaker. *The Family Crucible.* New York: Harper & Row, 1978.

Neil, John R., and David P. Kniskern, eds. *From Psyche to System: The Evolving Therapy of Carl Whitaker.* New York: Guilford Press, 1982.

Neugarten, Bernice L., ed. *Middle Age and Aging.* Chicago: University of Chicago Press, 1968.

O'Leary, Virginia E., and James M. Donoghue. "Latitudes of Masculinity: Reaction to Sex-Role Deviance in Men." *Journal of Social Issues* 34 (1978), pp. 17–28.

Paine, Robert. "In Search of Friendship: An Exploratory Analysis in Middle-Class Culture." *Journal of the Royal Anthropological Institute* 4 (1969), pp. 505–524.

Parlee, Mary Brown, et al. "The Friendship Bond." *Psychology Today* 13 (1979), pp. 43–54, 113–114.

Pietropinto, Anthony, and Jacqueline Simenauer. *Husbands and Wives.* New York: Berkley Books, 1981.

Pleck, Joseph H. "Man to Man: Is Brotherhood Possible?" In Nona Glazer-Malbin, ed. *Old Family/New Family.* New York: D. Van Nostrand, 1975.

———. *The Myth of Masculinity.* Cambridge, Mass.: MIT Press, 1981.

———, and Robert Brannon, eds. "Male Roles and the Male Experience." *Journal of Social Issues* 34 (1978), pp. 1–195.

———, and Jack Sawyer, eds. *Men and Masculinity.* Englewood Cliffs, N.J.: Prentice-Hall, 1974.

Poster, Mark. *Critical Theory of the Family.* New York: Seabury Press, 1978.

Powers, Edward A., and Gordon L. Bultena. "Sex Differences in Intimate Friendships in Old Age." *Journal of Marriage and the Family* 38 (1976), pp. 739–747.

Radcliffe-Brown, A. R., and Daryll Forde, eds. *African Systems of Kinship and Marriage.* London: Oxford University Press, 1950.

Rake, Johan Michele. "Friendship: A Fundamental Description of Its Subjective Dimension." *Humanitas* 6 (1970), pp. 161–176.

Rangell, Leo. "On Friendship." *Journal of the American Psychoanalytic Association* 11 (1963), pp. 3–54.

Reisman, John M. *Anatomy of Friendship.* New York: Irvington Publishers, 1979.

———, and Susan I. Shorr. "Friendship Claims and Expectations Among Children and Adults." *Child Development* 49 (1978), pp. 913–916.

Riesman, David, Nathan Glazer, Reuel Denney. *The Lonely Crowd.* Garden City, N.Y.: Doubleday Anchor, 1956.

Riley, Matilda White, Marilyn Johnson and Anne Foner. *Aging and Society.* New York: Russell Sage Foundation, 1972.

Robertiello, Richard C. *A Man in the Making.* New York: Richard Marek, 1979.

Rohrlich, Jay B. *Work and Love: The Crucial Balance.* New York: Summit Books, 1980.

Rose, Peter I., ed. *Socialization and the Life Cycle.* New York: St. Martin's Press, 1979.

Rosow, Irving. *Social Integration of the Aged.* New York: Free Press, 1967.

Rossi, Alice S. "Feminist Friendship." In *The Feminist Papers: Adams to Beauvoir.* New York: Columbia University Press, 1973.

Rubin, Lillian B. *Busing & Backlash: White Against White in an Urban School District.* Berkeley: University of California Press, 1972.

———. *Worlds of Pain: Life in the Working-Class Family.* New York: Basic Books, 1976.

———. *Women of a Certain Age: The Midlife Search for Self.* New York: Harper & Row, 1979.

———. *Intimate Strangers: Men and Women Together.* New York: Harper & Row, 1983.

Rubin, Zick. *Liking and Loving: An Invitation to Social Psychology.* New York: Holt, Rinehart and Winston, 1973.

———. *Children's Friendships.* Cambridge, Mass.: Harvard University Press, 1980.

Sadler, William A., Jr. "The Experience of Friendship." *Humanitas* 6 (1970), pp. 177–209.

Safilios-Rothschild, Constantina. *Love, Sex and Sex Roles.* Englewood Cliffs, N.J.: Prentice-Hall, 1977.

Satir, Virginia. *Conjoint Family Therapy.* Palo Alto: Science and Behavior Books, 1967.

———, James Stachowiak, Harvey Taschman. *Helping Families to Change.* New York: Jason Aronson, 1975.

Sattel, Jack W. "The Inexpressive Male: Tragedy or Sexual Politics?" *Social Problems* 23 (1976), pp. 469–477.

Schneider, David M. *American Kinship: A Cultural Account.* Englewood Cliffs, N.J.: Prentice-Hall, 1968.

Seiden, Anne M., and Pauline B. Bart. "Woman to Woman: Is Sisterhood Powerful?" In Nona Glazer-Malbin, ed. *Old Family/New Family.* New York: D. Van Nostrand, 1975.

Selman, Robert L., and Anne P. Selman. "Children's Ideas About Friendship: A New Theory." *Psychology Today* 13 (1979), pp. 71–80, 114.

Sennett, Richard. *Families Against the City.* Cambridge, Mass.: Harvard University Press, 1970.

———, and Jonathan Cobb. *Hidden Injuries of Class.* New York: Vintage Books, 1973.

Sorbin, Lisa A., Illene J. Tonick and Sarah Sternglanz. "Shaping Cooperative Cross-Sex Play." *Child Development* 48 (1977), pp. 924–929.

Sherfey, Mary Jane. *The Nature and Evolution of Female Sexuality.* New York: Vintage Books, 1973.

Shostak, Arthur B. *Blue-Collar Life.* New York: Random House, 1969.

Shulman, Norman. "Life Cycle Variations in Patterns of Close Relationships." *Journal of Marriage and the Family* 37 (1975), pp. 813–821.

Skolnick, Arlene S. *The Intimate Environment: Exploring Marriage and the Family.* Third edition. Boston: Little, Brown, 1983a.

———. "Parents, Peers and Partners: Stability and Change in Attachments from Infancy Through Middle Age." Unpublished paper presented to the Annual Meetings of the American Sociological Association, 1983b.

Smith, Joel, William H. Form and Gregory P. Stone. "Local Intimacy in a Middle-Sized City." *American Journal of Sociology* 60 (1954), pp. 276–284.

Smith-Rosenberg, Carroll. "The Female World of Love and Ritual: Relations Between Women in Nineteenth-Century America." *Signs* 1 (1975), pp. 1–29.

Spitz, René A. *The First Year of Life.* New York: International Universities Press, 1965.

Stein, Peter J., ed. *Single Life.* New York: St. Martin's Press, 1981.

Stueve, Ann, and Claude S. Fischer. "Social Networks and Older Women." Unpublished paper presented to the Workshop on Older Women, Washington, D.C., 1978.

———, and Kathleen Gerson. "Personal Relations Across the Life Cycle." In Claude S. Fischer et al. *Networks and Places: Social Relations in the Urban Setting.* New York: Free Press, 1977.

Sullivan, Harry Stack. *The Interpersonal Theory of Psychiatry.* New York: W. W. Norton, 1953.

Sutcliffe, J. P., and B. D. Crabbe. "Incidence and Degrees of Friendship in Urban and Rural Areas." *Social Forces* 42 (1963), pp. 60–67.

Taylor, Jeremy. *A Discourse on Friendship.* Cedar Rapids, Iowa: Torch Press, 1913.

Thomas, Alexander, and Stella Chess. *Temperament and Development.* New York: Brunner/Mazel, 1977.

Tiger, Lionel. *Men in Groups.* New York: Random House, 1969.

Tognoli, Jerome. "Male Friendship and Intimacy Across the Life Span." *Family Relations* 29 (1980), pp. 273–279.

Tufte, Virginia, and Barbara Myerhoff, eds. *Changing Images of the Family.* New Haven: Yale University Press, 1979.

Twain, Mark. "Pudd'nhead Wilson's Calendar." *Pudd'nhead Wilson.* New York: New American Library, 1964.

Useem, Michael. "Ideological and Interpersonal Change in the Radical Protest Movement." *Social Problems* 19 (1972), pp. 451–469.

Vaillant, George E. *Adaptation to Life.* Boston: Little, Brown, 1977.

Waters, Everett, Judith Wippman and L. Alan Sroufe. "Attachment, Positive Affect and Competence in the Peer Group." *Child Development* 50 (1979), pp. 821–829.

Weiss, Lawrence, and Marjorie Fiske Lowenthal. "Life Course Perspectives on Friendship." In Marjorie Fiske Lowenthal, Majda Thurnher and David Chiriboga. *Four Stages of Life.* San Francisco: Jossey-Bass, 1975.

Weiss, Robert S. *Marital Separation.* New York: Basic Books, 1975.

———. *Going It Alone.* New York: Basic Books, 1979.

———, ed. *Loneliness: The Experience of Emotional and Social Isolation.* Cambridge, Mass.: MIT Press, 1973.

West, Candace. "When the Doctor Is a 'Lady': Power, Status and Gender in Physician-Patient Encounters." *Symbolic Interaction* 7 (1984), pp. 87–106.

Whitten, Norman E. "Network Analysis in Ecuador and Nova Scotia." *Canadian Review of Sociology and Anthropology* 7 (1970), pp. 269–280.

Winnicott, D. W. *The Family and Individual Development.* New York: Basic Books, 1965a.

———. *The Maturational Processes and the Facilitating Environment.* New York: International Universities Press, 1965b.

———. *Playing and Reality.* London: Tavistock Publications, 1971.

Wolf, Eric R. "Kinship, Friendship and Patron-Client Relations in Complex Societies." In Michael Banton, ed. *The Social Anthropology of Complex Societies.* London: Tavistock Publications, 1966.

Wolfe, Alvin W. "On Structural Comparisons of Networks." *Canadian Review of Sociology and Anthropology* 7 (1970), 226–244.

Wood, Vivian, and Joan F. Robertson. "Friendship and Kinship Interaction; Differential Effect on the Morale of the Elderly." *Journal of Marriage and the Family* 40 (1978), pp. 367–375.

Yankelovich, Daniel. *New Rules: Searching for Fulfillment in a World Turned Upside Down.* New York: Random House, 1981.

Young, Michael, and Peter Willmott. *Family and Kinship in East London.* Baltimore: Penguin Books, 1962.

Zaretsky, Eli. *Capitalism, the Family and Personal Life.* New York: Harper Colophon, 1976.

Zilbergeld, Bernie. *Male Sexuality.* Boston: Little, Brown, 1978.

Index